SHARKS
AND OTHER DEADLY
OCEAN CREATURES

VISUAL ENCYCLOPEDIA

CONTENTS

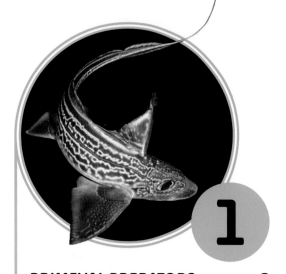

1

2

MUSCLE-MOUTHED GULPERS 90

CRUISERS AND CHASERS 104

PREDATOR POWER

This scale depends on prey size and the possible danger a predator poses to humans.

Predators that feed on planktonic animals; also parasites that may not kill their victims.

Predators that target small invertebrates and small fish, up to the size of mackerel.

Predators that target and kill medium-sized prey, bigger than mackerel.

Predators that kill small or medium-sized prey, but have venom that could kill bigger animals.

Predators that target large prey up to the size of big mammals, potentially humans.

SCALES AND SIZES

Profiles of sharks and other creatures have scale drawings to indicate their size.

 8 in (20.3 cm)   6 ft (1.8 m)   6 ft (1.8 m)

7

8

1 PRIMEVAL PREDATORS

Sharks first swam the oceans well before the time of the dinosaurs, but other meat-eaters have hunted in these waters even longer. Some prehistoric predators, such as reptilian ichthyosaurs, were quite different from creatures alive today, but others were the ancestors of living animals, including sharks. A few primeval predators, such as the frilled shark, still lurk in the ocean depths.

SEA LAMPREY

Petromyzon marinus

Lampreys are jawless fish that have scarcely changed in hundreds of millions of years. Like most other lampreys, the adult sea lamprey—the biggest of all—is a blood-sucking parasite of other fish. Adults migrate into rivers to breed, where their eggs hatch into a kind of filter-feeding larva called an ammocoete—found only in lampreys.

DATA FILE

PREDATOR POWER

SIZE: Up to 35.4 in (90 cm) long

DISTRIBUTION: Coastal waters of North Atlantic Ocean and western Mediterranean Sea

DIET: Larvae are filter-feeders; adults feed as parasites on blood of other fish

Rings of pointed, hornlike teeth scrape at the side of prey to draw blood

Sucker-like, jawless mouth clamps on to side of fish

Sea lamprey, side view

The sea lamprey may **sometimes attack whales** or dolphins.

DEVONIAN PLACODERM

Dunkleosteus sp.

***Dunkleosteus*, side view**

Hinged connection between head and body

Dunkleosteus's **bite strength** may have rivaled that of a great white shark.

Massive, sharp jaws had the strength to bite through prey that had thick armor

The armor-plated placoderms were among the first vertebrates with biting jaws, and so were the first predators to dominate the oceans before the evolution of modern sharks. Their jaws actually worked more like a giant beak. Massive *Dunkleosteus*, known from its fossilized head and body shields, was an early top predator from the Devonian Period (419–358 MYA).

DATA FILE

 PREDATOR POWER

SIZE: Up to 19.7 ft (6 m) long

DISTRIBUTION: Oceans and seas in areas now in North America, Europe, and northern Africa

DIET: Fish and large invertebrates, including those with armor

DEVONIAN
SHARK
Cladoselache sp.

This small-toothed shark may have **swallowed prey whole**.

Cladoselache belongs to a group of prehistoric sharks that existed in the Devonian Period (419–358 MYA) and which became extinct well before modern sharks evolved. They had some features that set them apart from later sharks, such as sparsely-scaled skin, but they were formidable ocean hunters, and could swim at great speed.

DEVONIAN
SHARK
Stethacanthus sp.

Anvil-shaped "spine brush"

The remarkable "spine brush" on the back of this early shark from the Devonian Period was made up of a tight bundle of hard, mineralized rods that seemed to spring from the base of the front dorsal fin. The fact that only male sharks had this structure may mean its purpose was to attract mates.

Spine in front of each dorsal fin

Smooth skin lacked the prickly denticles that make the skin of modern sharks rough like sandpaper

DATA FILE

PREDATOR POWER

SIZE: Up to 6.6 ft (2 m) long

DISTRIBUTION: Oceans and seas in areas now in North America

DIET: Fish, as indicated by fossilized prey found in the stomach

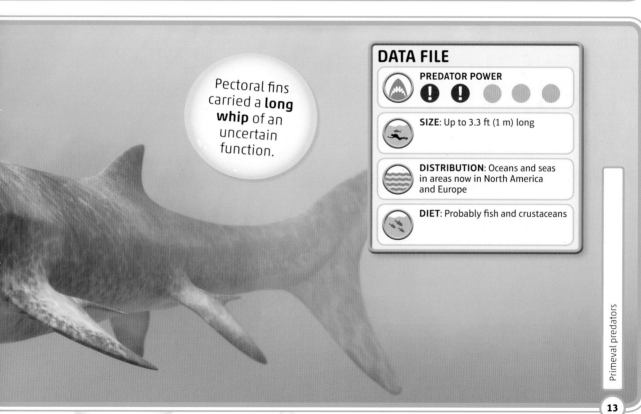

Pectoral fins carried a **long whip** of an uncertain function.

DATA FILE

PREDATOR POWER

SIZE: Up to 3.3 ft (1 m) long

DISTRIBUTION: Oceans and seas in areas now in North America and Europe

DIET: Probably fish and crustaceans

Primeval predators

CARBONIFEROUS
SHARK
Falcatus falcatus

Males and females of this shark from the Carboniferous Period (358–298 MYA) looked very different. Only males had the unusual, forward-pointing head spine. It had disproportionately big eyes, perhaps suggesting it was an active predator that relied on good vision to catch or ambush its prey in cloudy water.

PREHISTORIC EEL-LIKE
SHARK
Xenacanthus sp.

This shark's spine may have been **venomous**.

The long-bodied fossils of this fish show that it might have swum like an eel. This shark from the Permian Period (298–252 MYA) differed from all living sharks in that it had an elongated dorsal fin running along the length of its back, which was connected to the tail fin. Unusually for sharks, it seems to have lived in swampy areas rather than in the ocean.

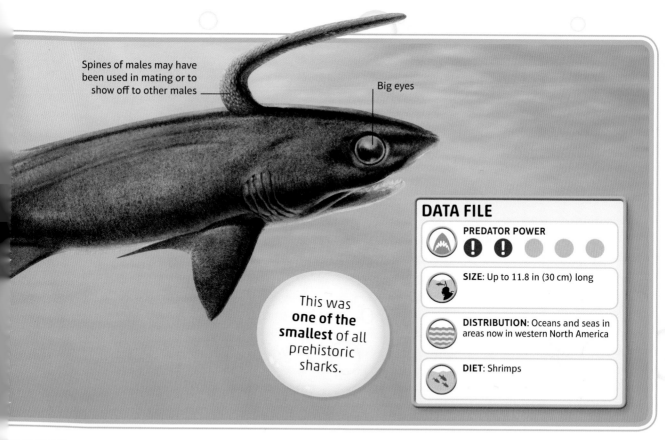

Spines of males may have been used in mating or to show off to other males

Big eyes

This was **one of the smallest** of all prehistoric sharks.

DATA FILE

PREDATOR POWER

SIZE: Up to 11.8 in (30 cm) long

DISTRIBUTION: Oceans and seas in areas now in western North America

DIET: Shrimps

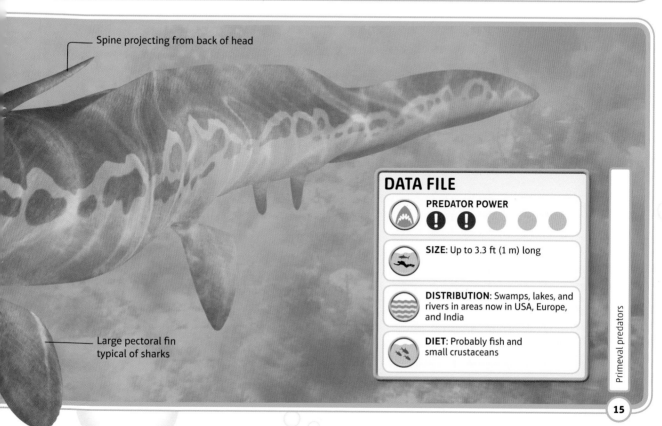

Spine projecting from back of head

Large pectoral fin typical of sharks

DATA FILE

PREDATOR POWER

SIZE: Up to 3.3 ft (1 m) long

DISTRIBUTION: Swamps, lakes, and rivers in areas now in USA, Europe, and India

DIET: Probably fish and small crustaceans

Primeval predators

HYBODONT SHARK

Hybodus sp.

Of all the sharks that appeared before the dinosaurs, *Hybodus*, from the Permian to Cretaceous Periods, was one of the most similar to modern sharks and its fossils are widespread. It had sharp front teeth for grabbing prey and blunter ones at the back for crunching, similar to modern snail-eating sharks.

Hybodus's skeleton was **more bone-like** than in other sharks.

Sharp spine in front of each dorsal fin, as in some modern sharks

Cutting and grinding teeth in large jaws for grasping and crushing prey

Torpedo-shaped body similar to modern sharks

DATA FILE

 PREDATOR POWER

 SIZE: Up to 6.6 ft (2 m) long

 DISTRIBUTION: Shallow seas and freshwaters worldwide

 DIET: Probably fish and invertebrates, including hard-shelled prey

SHARPNOSE
SEVENGILL SHARK
Heptranchias perlo

Large eyes

One of just two species of living sharks with seven gills (the other being the broadnose sevengill shark), this hunter is also one of the smallest of the living "primitive" sharks. The sharpnose sevengill spends much of its time in deep water, but is speedy enough to prey on other small sharks, and has enlarged eyes to help it see in dark water.

Seven gill slits unlike most sharks, which have five

The sharpnose sevengill is **known to bite** sometimes when caught.

DATA FILE

 PREDATOR POWER

 SIZE: Up to 4.6 ft (1.4 m) long

 DISTRIBUTION: Coastal waters of Atlantic, Indian, and Pacific oceans, and Mediterranean Sea

 DIET: Fish (including other small sharks), squid, and cuttlefish

BLUNTNOSE SIXGILL SHARK
Hexanchus griseus

Single dorsal fin near the rear, like in other primeval sharks

Six gill slits on the side of the body, unlike most sharks, which have five

This is one of the **most globally widespread** of all sharks.

The biggest living primeval shark, the bluntnose sixgill shuns the sunshine and sticks instead to deep, darker waters. It stays close to the bottom and usually only rises upward at night. Sometimes it follows migrating fish into shallow bays that are dimmed by blooms of plankton, grabbing the occasional seal along the way.

DATA FILE

PREDATOR POWER

SIZE: Up to 15.7 ft (4.8 m) long

DISTRIBUTION: Deep waters in oceans worldwide and Mediterranean Sea

DIET: Fish (including other sharks), squid, crustaceans, and sometimes seals

BROADNOSE
SEVENGILL SHARK
Notorynchus cepedianus

Blunt,
pointed snout

Broadnose sevengills team up and **work together** to hunt seals.

Dark spots are common, while some sharks may have white spots on darker backgrounds

Unlike other living primeval sharks, the broadnose sevengill likes to prowl along coastlines. Here, where the churned-up waters are murky, this hunter relies on poor visibility to take its prey by surprise. It even pokes its head out of the water to watch for prey, such as seals, closer to shore.

DATA FILE

 PREDATOR POWER

SIZE: Up to 9.8 ft (3 m) long

 DISTRIBUTION: Temperate coastal waters of the Americas, South Africa, Asia, and Australasia

 DIET: Fish (including other sharks), seals, and dolphins

Primeval predators

FRILLED SHARK

Chlamydoselachus anguineus

This shark has green eyes, like many others found in deep water

The frilled shark resembles a storybook serpent. It swims slowly by rippling its long body, but stays in deep, dark water, so is rarely seen alive. Its mouth is filled with three-pronged teeth that may act like little grappling hooks for grabbing slippery prey, such as squid.

First gill slits meet under the head to form a frill

SPIRAL-TOOTHED CHIMEROID

Helicoprion sp.

Scientists **X-rayed fossils** to work out this hunter's anatomy.

This prehistoric relative of living chimaeras had a spiral blade in the floor of its mouth. The "tooth-whorl" on this blade probably spun backward as the lower jaw closed, but fossils show no wear on teeth. This suggests that *Helicoprion* fed on soft-bodied prey, such as squid.

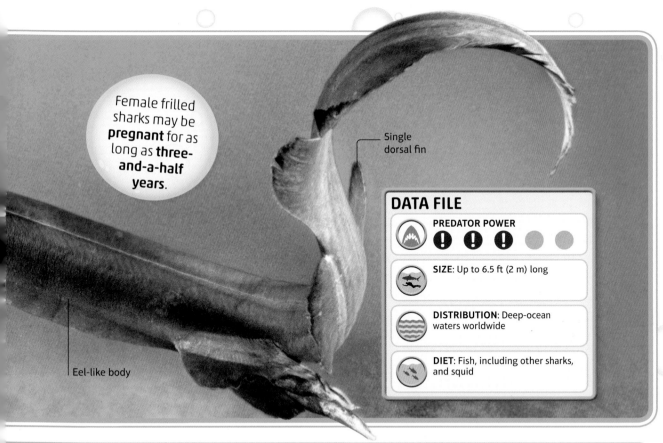

Female frilled sharks may be **pregnant** for as long as **three-and-a-half years**.

Single dorsal fin

Eel-like body

DATA FILE

PREDATOR POWER

SIZE: Up to 6.5 ft (2 m) long

DISTRIBUTION: Deep-ocean waters worldwide

DIET: Fish, including other sharks, and squid

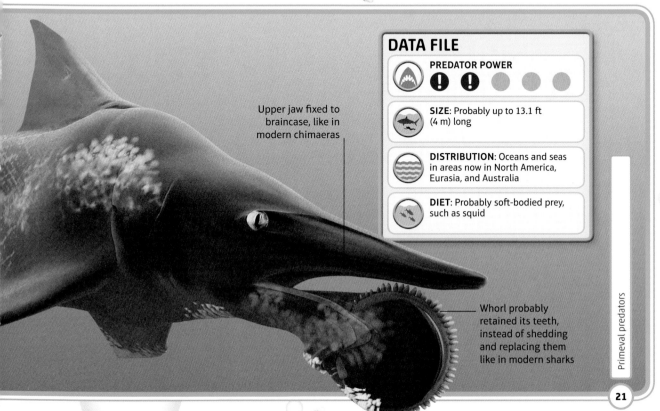

Upper jaw fixed to braincase, like in modern chimaeras

DATA FILE

PREDATOR POWER

SIZE: Probably up to 13.1 ft (4 m) long

DISTRIBUTION: Oceans and seas in areas now in North America, Eurasia, and Australia

DIET: Probably soft-bodied prey, such as squid

Whorl probably retained its teeth, instead of shedding and replacing them like in modern sharks

CARBONIFEROUS
SPINY "SHARK"
Acanthodes sp.

Spiny "sharks," from the Carboniferous Period (358–298 MYA), had strong spines to support their fins. However, these were not true sharks. Their spines were made of bone, suggesting that the animals might have been related to bony fish, rather than to cartilaginous sharks. They also lacked teeth, so they probably filtered plankton rather than biting prey.

Body covered in tiny scales

CRETACEOUS
CHIMAERA
Ischyodus bifurcatus

Like living chimaeras, males had a long projection (tentaculum) for grasping females during mating

Even though this fish swam in the oceans in the Cretaceous Period (145–66 MYA), it was remarkably similar to the modern ratfish, a related chimaera that is common in oceans today. This suggests that, as a group, chimaeras have changed very little in more than 70 million years of evolution.

Primeval predators

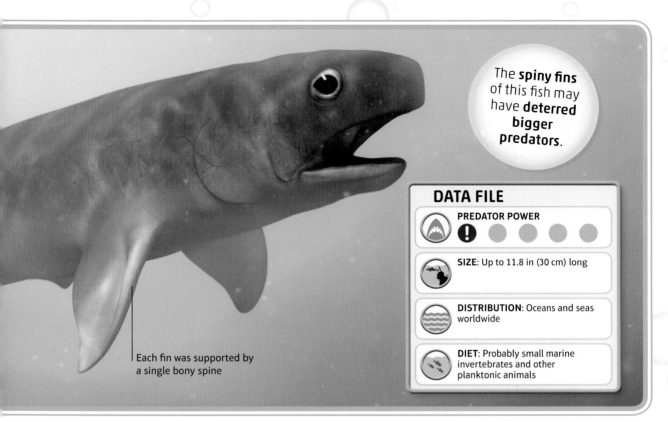

The **spiny fins** of this fish may have **deterred bigger predators**.

DATA FILE

PREDATOR POWER
❗ ● ● ● ●

SIZE: Up to 11.8 in (30 cm) long

DISTRIBUTION: Oceans and seas worldwide

DIET: Probably small marine invertebrates and other planktonic animals

Each fin was supported by a single bony spine

Some species of *Ischyodus* **lived** almost **to the present day**.

Long, tapering, ratlike tail

DATA FILE

PREDATOR POWER
❗ ❗ ● ● ●

SIZE: Up to 3.3 ft (1 m) long

DISTRIBUTION: Oceans and seas in areas now in North America

DIET: Probably hard-shelled invertebrates, such as mollusks and crustaceans

Primeval predators

AUSTRALIAN PLOUGHNOSE
CHIMAERA

Callorhinchus milii

Shimmering skin

Big pectoral fins flap like wings and propel the fish

Hoe-shaped snout is packed with sensors for detecting buried prey

Chimaeras' toothplates are not shed like shark teeth, but **keep growing**.

Most chimaeras are deep-water fish, but this one prefers to swim in the shallower waters along coastlines. The Australian ploughnose chimaera uses its peculiar, hoe-shaped snout to probe the mud and sense the activity of buried, hard-shelled, invertebrate prey. It is sometimes called a ghost shark because of its shimmery skin.

DATA FILE

 PREDATOR POWER

 SIZE: Up to 4.3 ft (1.3 m) long

 DISTRIBUTION: Coastal ocean waters around southern Australia and New Zealand

 DIET: Mainly mollusks, such as clams, and other bottom-living invertebrates

PACIFIC LONGNOSE
CHIMAERA
Rhinochimaera pacifica

Spear-shaped snout is half the length of the body

This bizarre-looking hunter is little known and is usually seen only as a curiosity when fishing nets are brought to the surface. The precise purpose of this chimaera's long, spear-shaped snout is not well understood, but, like other chimaeras, its sensors probably help this bottom-living fish find buried invertebrate prey.

Broad, winglike, pectoral fins

Gill openings are covered by a flap called an operculum, as in all chimaeras

This chimaera lives in **deep-ocean troughs**.

DATA FILE

 PREDATOR POWER
 ❗ ❗ ⬤ ⬤ ⬤

 SIZE: Up to 5.2 ft (1.6 m) long

 DISTRIBUTION: Deep-ocean waters around Japan, East Asia, Australasia, and Peru

 DIET: Probably hard-shelled invertebrates, such as crabs and mollusks

RABBITFISH

Chimaera monstrosa

The rabbitfish belongs to a group of fish called chimaeras. Like in sharks, their skeleton is made from cartilage. However, they split away from sharks and rays over 100 million years before dinosaurs appeared. They differ in having a protective shield, called an operculum, covering their gill opening, and grinding tooth-plates, instead of cutting blades, to crush their prey.

Long, mildly-venomous dorsal fin spine inflicts painful wound

Large eyes to see in deep, dark waters

Snout packed with sensors to help detect bottom-living prey

DATA FILE

PREDATOR POWER

SIZE: Up to 4.9 ft (1.5 m) long

DISTRIBUTION: Coastal waters of north-western Atlantic Ocean and Mediterranean Sea

DIET: Mainly hard-shelled invertebrates, such as crabs and mollusks

Like sharks, male chimaeras have a clasper to help introduce sperm into the female during mating

The tooth-plates of this chimaera **may project from its mouth,** like in a rabbit.

GIANT JURASSIC
BONY FISH
Leedsichthys problematicus

The mega-sized *Leedsichthys* was a bony fish, rather than a cartilaginous shark, but its lifestyle was probably similar to the unrelated, modern-day whale shark. Its huge mouth contained gill-rakers for straining small animals from the ocean water. So, like the whale shark, this giant from the Jurassic Period (201–145 MYA) was a gentle filter-feeder.

Enormous set of spiny gill-rakers in mouth filtered plankton

ALLIGATOR
GAR
Atractosteus spatula

Dorsal fin set far back on long body

Hardened, diamond-shaped scales, like those found only in certain primitive groups of bony fish

One of the biggest fish of North America's swamps, the alligator gar is a formidable ambush predator. While it grabs prey using the double lining of sharp teeth in its jaws, the hardened scales on its body act like armor to protect it from attacks from other animals. It can even breathe in air to supplement the oxygen it gets from the water.

DATA FILE

PREDATOR POWER
(!) ( ) ( ) ( ) ( )

SIZE: Up to 55.8 ft (17 m) long

DISTRIBUTION: Oceans and seas in areas now in Europe and South America

DIET: Probably planktonic animals, such as small fish and invertebrates

Long, scythe-shaped pectoral fins

Leedsichthys was the **largest bony fish** that has ever existed.

DATA FILE

PREDATOR POWER
(!) (!) (!) ( ) ( )

SIZE: up to 8.2 ft (2.5 m) long

DISTRIBUTION: Lakes, swamps, rivers, estuaries, and coastal bays of southern USA and northern Mexico

DIET: Mainly fish and sometimes birds and small mammals swimming at the surface

Some fossils of this fish date back to **100 million years ago**.

Primeval predators

COELACANTH

Latimeria chalumnae

When the first coelacanth was discovered among a fisherman's catch in 1938, it caused a sensation. Before this find, scientists thought this kind of fish had become extinct with the dinosaurs. Together with the lung fish, the coelacanth is one of just a few fish alive today to have the kind of fleshy "lobe-fins" that helped the first vertebrates to conquer land.

Coelacanths have **not changed much** in 390 million years.

Body covered in "armor" of unusually tough scales

Peculiar, three-lobed tail fin found in very few other kinds of fish

Fleshy, lobe-like pelvic fins

DATA FILE

 PREDATOR POWER

 SIZE: Up to 6.6 ft (2 m) long

 DISTRIBUTION: Deep waters and rocky caves of western Indian Ocean

 DIET: Fish

CRETACEOUS
PLESIOSAUR
Albertonectes vanderveldei

The prehistoric oceans were home to two main groups of marine reptiles— the ichthyosaurs and the plesiosaurs. Unlike the ichthyosaurs, the plesiosaurs swallowed stones to counteract the buoyancy of their lungs. They might have done this so they could rest on the ocean floor to grab passing prey. Many plesiosaurs had a long neck to help them swipe at shoals of fish—and *Albertonectes* had the longest neck of them all.

Albertonectes had **76 vertebrae** in its neck.

Neck was 23 ft (7 m) long

Two pairs of flippers propelled the animal

Small, pointed teeth probably grabbed soft-bodied prey

DATA FILE

 PREDATOR POWER

 SIZE: Up to 59.1 ft (18 m) long

 DISTRIBUTION: Oceans and seas in areas now in North America

 DIET: Probably fish and soft-bodied, swimming invertebrates

Primeval predators

JURASSIC
ICHTHYOSAUR
Stenopterygius sp.

The ichthyosaurs of the Jurassic Period (201–145 MYA) were among the first big groups of predatory marine vertebrates to breathe air. *Stenopterygius* and other ichthyosaurs would keep coming to the water surface to breathe. These reptiles evolved as dolphin-shaped fish-eaters with a fishlike tail. Unlike most other reptiles, they gave birth to live young in the water.

Stenopterygius could probably swim as **fast as a modern-day tuna**.

Single dorsal fin

Long, pointed snout, filled with sharp teeth for grabbing slippery prey

Two pairs of flippers for swimming

DATA FILE

 PREDATOR POWER
 ❗ ❗ ❗

 SIZE: Up to 13.1 ft (4 m) long

 DISTRIBUTION: Oceans and seas in areas now in Europe

 DIET: Fish and belemnoids (prehistoric relatives of modern squid)

MEGALODON
Carcharodon megalodon

Teeth could have been up to five times bigger than those of the great white

Torpedo-shaped body for speedy swimming

Megalodon may have had the **biggest bite force** of any animal.

The largest shark that ever lived appeared in the Miocene epoch (23–5 MYA), a time when mammals had long since replaced dinosaurs. *Megalodon* was a relatively modern cousin of the great white shark, rather than a genuinely primeval predator. It probably evolved to hunt the whales that had begun to appear in the oceans at that time.

DATA FILE

PREDATOR POWER
! ! ! ! !

SIZE: Possibly more than 65.6 ft (20 m) long

DISTRIBUTION: Oceans and seas worldwide

DIET: Large fish and marine mammals such as whales

2
MUD-ROOTING MONSTERS

Most sharks hunt in the ocean's mid-waters, but some, including angelsharks, have a different lifestyle. They have flat bodies that hug the seabed, skin colors that match their background, and rely on camouflage to catch their prey. Virtually all rays, the closest living relatives of sharks, have made their living this way. Some bony fishes, such as flatfish, are bottom-dwellers too.

LONGNOSE SAWSHARK

Pristiophorus cirratus

Sawsharks use their swordlike snout for both sensing and killing prey. The snout is packed with sensors that detect the muscular activity of small animals buried in sand and gravel. Once the prey is roused from its hiding place, the sawshark sweeps its snout from side to side, cutting the unfortunate victim to pieces.

Long, swordlike snout has 19–21 large teeth running along each side

DATA FILE

 PREDATOR POWER

 SIZE: Up to 4.9 ft (1.5 m) long

 DISTRIBUTION: Shallow coastal waters of western and southern Australia

 DIET: Small fish and crustaceans

The shark's barbels let it **"taste" prey** hidden in sand.

Brownish body may have darker, faint blotches

Dark brown lines run down each side of the snout

Sensory barbels

SAND DEVIL

Squatina dumeril

Angelsharks are named for their broad pectoral fins, which look like angel's wings. Their behavior, however, is anything but angelic. When disturbed, the sand devil bites aggressively with its needlelike teeth. In northern parts of its range, it moves inshore close to the coast, but further south it sticks to deeper water.

Plain, gray body may have some darker spots

One of two small dorsal fins near the tail fin

The sand devil gets its name from its **aggressive temperament**.

DATA FILE

 PREDATOR POWER
  ● ● ●

 SIZE: Up to 4.9 ft (1.5 m) long

 DISTRIBUTION: Coastal waters of western North America and Caribbean Sea

 DIET: Bottom-living fish, crustaceans, and bivalve mollusks, such as clams and mussels

38

COMMON ANGELSHARK
Squatina squatina

Angelsharks look and behave like rays. When prey passes nearby, however, they turn into formidable hunters. They make a grab with lightning-fast jaws, and can even arch their "neck" upward to help with the catch. This species is found only in Europe, but other angelsharks are found around the world.

White, crisscrossing lines disappear as the shark grows bigger

This shark can strike its prey in **one-tenth of a second**.

Grayish or brownish body peppered with spots

DATA FILE

 PREDATOR POWER

 SIZE: Up to 5.9 ft (1.8 m) long

 DISTRIBUTION: Shallow coastal waters of Europe and Mediterranean Sea

 DIET: Bottom-living fish (especially flatfish and skates), crustaceans, and mollusks

Mud-rooting monsters

BIG SKATE
Raja binoculata

Young skates follow **any moving object**, not just their mother.

Two tiny dorsal fins set far back on tapering tail

One of two eyelike spots on the upper surface of the skate's body gives it the scientific name *binoculata*

Skates make up nearly half of the hundreds of species of rays. The big skate is the biggest one in the waters around North America. Its rigid, pointed snout and triangular "wings" give it the shape of a diamond that is as wide as it is long. It glides gracefully when swimming, but spends more time partly buried in the mud, with just its eyes poking out.

DATA FILE

 PREDATOR POWER

 SIZE: Up to 7.9 ft (2.4 m) long

DISTRIBUTION: Coastal waters of western North America

  DIET: Fish and crustaceans

COMMON
GUITARFISH
Rhinobatos rhinobatos

Guitarfish have high dorsal fins, like sharks, but a flattened, ray-like body. They are more closely related to rays and share their habit of hunting buried animals. The common guitarfish pins down shrimps and other prey on the seabed with its pointed snout, before sucking them into its mouth and crushing them with its molar-like teeth.

DATA FILE

 PREDATOR POWER

SIZE: Up to 4.9 ft (1.5 m) long

DISTRIBUTION: Coastal waters over mud or sand of Mediterranean Sea and eastern Atlantic Ocean

DIET: Bottom-living invertebrates and fish

A **milk-like liquid** inside the mother's womb nourishes unborn pups.

One of two dorsal fins near the rear of the body

Pectoral fins form "wings" on guitar-shaped body

GIANT
GUITARFISH

Rhynchobatus djiddensis

The dorsal fins of this guitarfish are bigger and more sharklike than those of the related wedgefish, and its pointed snout is longer. When hunting in muddy shallows, the giant guitarfish often comes right up into the surf, making it an easy catch for fishermen. Because it breeds slowly and has a small litter size, over-fished populations take time to recover.

DATA FILE

 PREDATOR POWER

 SIZE: Up to 10.2 ft (3.1 m) long

 DISTRIBUTION: Coral reefs and estuaries of Red Sea and Indian Ocean

 DIET: Crabs, lobsters, bivalves, squid, and small fish

White spots on a brown-gray background

Females give birth to a small litter of **just four pups**.

Sharply pointed snout

SMALL-TOOTHED SAWFISH

Pristis pectinata

This sawfish often swims into the **mouths of rivers**.

Long snout edged with row of teeth running along each side

Eyes much smaller than those of sawsharks

Although this sawfish is similar to sawsharks, its downward-facing gill slits show that it is more closely related to rays. Like the sawsharks, the small-toothed sawfish uses its "saw" as a sense organ as well as a weapon. It sweeps its saw to impale small fish and then scrapes off the injured prey on the sea bottom to eat it.

DATA FILE

 PREDATOR POWER

 SIZE: Up to 24.9 ft (7.6 m) long

 DISTRIBUTION: Coastal waters and estuaries of Atlantic, Indian, and Pacific oceans

 DIET: Fish and shellfish

Mud-rooting monsters

MARBLED
TORPEDO RAY
Torpedo marmorata

The torpedo ray stuns prey by firing electric shocks into the water, but it also uses the shocks for self-defense. It arches its belly outward to make the shock spread out more effectively. It generates up to 200 volts, enough to knock another fish senseless or give a painful jolt to a human.

DATA FILE

 PREDATOR POWER

 SIZE: Up to 3.3 ft (1 m) long

 DISTRIBUTION: Coastal waters over reefs and seagrass of eastern Atlantic Ocean and Mediterranean Sea

DIET: Bottom-living fish and invertebrates

Round dorsal fins over tail

Marbled pattern camouflages this ray from prey on sea bottom

The electric shock organs of this ray develop **even before they are born**.

LESSER ELECTRIC RAY

Narcine bancroftii

DATA FILE

 PREDATOR POWER

 SIZE: Up to 23.6 in (60 cm) long

 DISTRIBUTION: Tropical coastal waters of western Atlantic Ocean and Caribbean Sea

DIET: Mainly marine worms

This species belongs to a family of electric rays that are sometimes called numbfish. Numbfish are generally smaller than the related torpedo rays and give weaker electric shocks, more in self-defense, rather than to stun prey. As in torpedo rays, the jaws of the lesser electric ray protrude from its head to grab prey buried in mud and silt.

Rays may use electric shocks **to communicate with one another**.

Snout more pointed than that of torpedo rays

Mud-rooting monsters

BLUE-SPOTTED
RIBBONTAIL RAY
Taeniura lymma

The strikingly colored blue-spotted ribbontail ray often rests among rocks or stays buried in sand with just its eyes and sting-bearing tail showing. The sting has one or two backward-pointing, venomous spines that can inflict a painful injury when used in self-defense. Like other rays, this fish smothers bottom-living prey with its flat, disklike body before eating them.

Small, prickly denticles run down the back

Bright blue spots may help disguise the ray in sun-dappled, shallow water

Sting is further back on tail than is the case with most other kinds of stingray

Skin is mostly smooth

This ray's **venomous spines** are up to **2.7 in (7 cm) long**.

DATA FILE

PREDATOR POWER
! ! ! !

SIZE: Up to 27.5 in (70 cm) long

DISTRIBUTION: Coral reef and sand flats of Red Sea, and tropical Indian and west Pacific oceans

DIET: Mollusks, worms, shrimps, and crabs

Mud-rooting monsters

PEACOCK
FLOUNDER
Bothus mancus

Both eyes on left side in this left-eyed flatfish

The peacock flounder is a flatfish that can change color to match its surroundings. Like other flatfish, the young that hatch from eggs look unremarkable. As they grow, they go through a process of physical change whereby their eyes end up on one side of the body. The fish settles down on the seabed with its eyeless side flat on the bottom.

LESSER
WEEVER
Echiichthys vipera

Dorsal fin spines are connected to venom glands

Eyes on top of head peer upward to look out for passing prey

The lesser weever is a particular hazard for anyone walking barefoot on a sandy beach. This little fish buries itself in the sand with just its eyes and dorsal fin poking up. It has sharp, stinging spines, and although the fish is scarcely the size of a goldfish, a sting from those spines can cause terrible pain.

Mud-rooting monsters

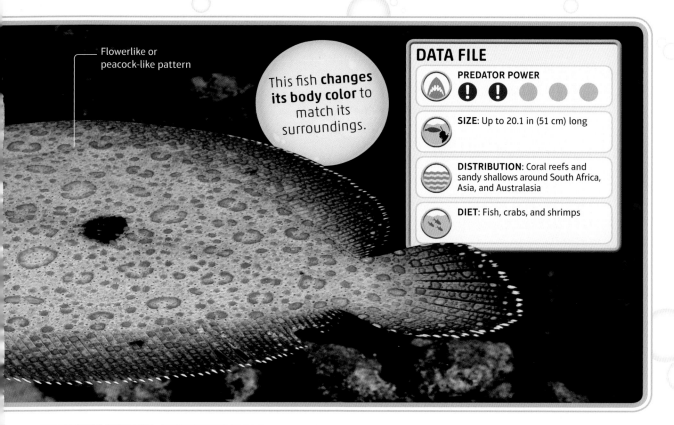

Flowerlike or peacock-like pattern

This fish **changes its body color** to match its surroundings.

DATA FILE

PREDATOR POWER
❗ ❗ ○ ○ ○

SIZE: Up to 20.1 in (51 cm) long

DISTRIBUTION: Coral reefs and sandy shallows around South Africa, Asia, and Australasia

DIET: Fish, crabs, and shrimps

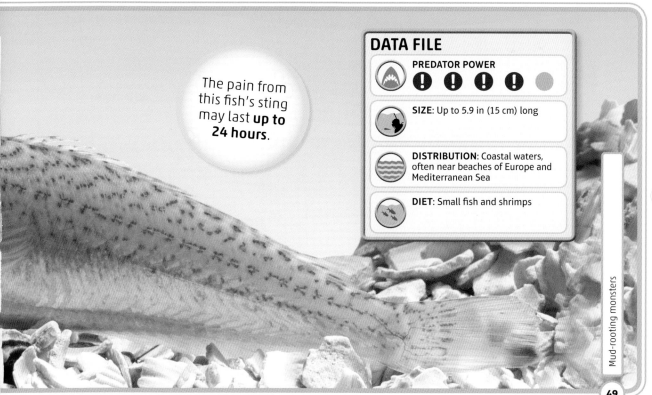

The pain from this fish's sting may last **up to 24 hours**.

DATA FILE

PREDATOR POWER
❗ ❗ ❗ ❗ ○

SIZE: Up to 5.9 in (15 cm) long

DISTRIBUTION: Coastal waters, often near beaches of Europe and Mediterranean Sea

DIET: Small fish and shrimps

Mud-rooting monsters

SAND STARGAZER
Dactyloscopus tridigitatus

The sand stargazer is one of the tiniest fish predators, but it has one of the best tricks for a perfect ambush. The fish gets its name because its eyes point upward on top of its head. This means it can keep practically its entire body buried in sand, while still keeping watch for any prey passing overhead.

Low dorsal fin on the back runs along the length of the body

Upward-pointing eyes

The male **guards eggs** in its **"armpits,"** under each pectoral fin.

Wide, upward-turned mouth

BITING REEF WORM

Eunice aphroditois

The biting reef worm grows up to 9.8 ft (3 m) and has jaws that can draw blood from a human finger. This giant waits in the sand, open-mouthed, with its head poking up into the water. When a fish swims within reach, the worm snaps its jaws shut, pulling the prey into its burrow.

Five antenne sense the presence of prey

Sharp-edged jaws can easily slice through fish

This worm's **can span** a distance of **1.9 in (5 cm).**

DATA FILE

PREDATOR POWER

SIZE: Up to 9.8 ft (3 m) long

DISTRIBUTION: Coastal mud and sand of Indian and western Pacific oceans

DIET: Fish, shrimps, other worms, seaweed, and dead matter

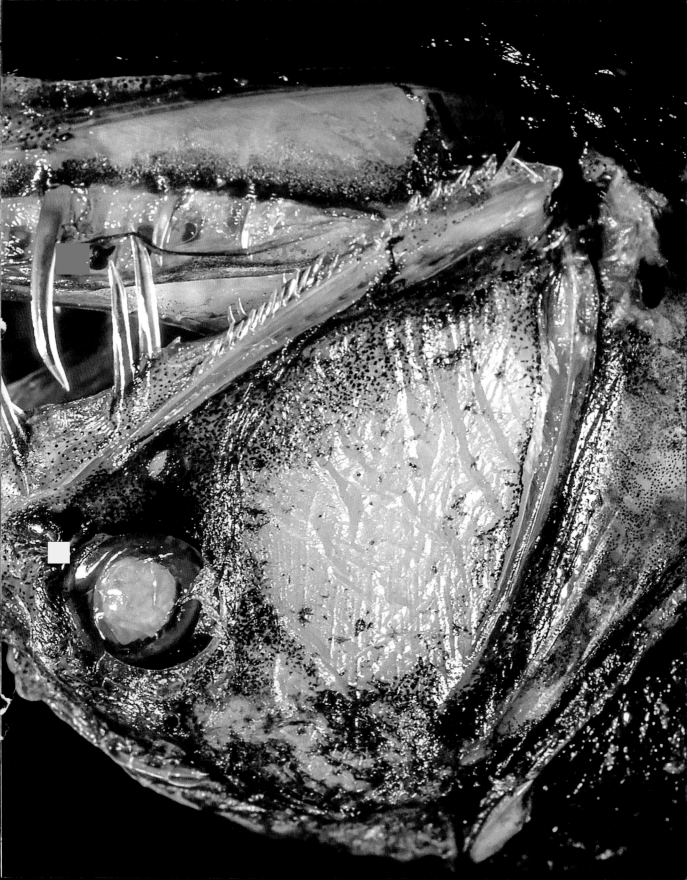

3
DEVILS OF THE DARK

The most well-known sharks, including the great white, chase their prey near the surface of the ocean. However, more mysterious kinds of predator hunt further down in darker depths. Some remarkable oddities live in this dark world. There are miniature sharks that give off glowing light, and even sneaky parasites that steal lumps of flesh from their unfortunate victims.

ANGULAR ROUGH SHARK
Oxynotus centrina

No other sharks look like rough sharks. This species, like other rough sharks, has high, sail-like dorsal fins—the first just behind the head. An especially oily liver helps to keep this small shark buoyant as it cruises slowly just above the ocean floor, close to its source of favorite food—bottom-living worms.

Rounded pelvic fin

VELVET-BELLY
Etmopterus spinax

The velvet-belly belongs to a group of small, deep-water hunters called lantern sharks. Light-producing organs, called "photophores," pepper the body surface of these sharks, glowing like little lanterns in the dark. They may help to dazzle prey or confuse bigger predators.

The velvet-belly produces **up to 21 pups** in a litter.

Brownish upper surface contrasts sharply with darker under surface

DATA FILE

PREDATOR POWER

SIZE: Up to 4.9 ft (1.5 m) long

DISTRIBUTION: Deep-coastal waters of eastern Atlantic Ocean and Mediterranean Sea

DIET: Mainly worms

This shark has especially rough, prickly skin.

Leaf-shaped pectoral fin

DATA FILE

PREDATOR POWER

SIZE: Up to 16.1 in (41 cm) long

DISTRIBUTION: Deep-ocean waters of eastern Atlantic Ocean and western Mediterranean Sea

DIET: Small fish, squid, and crustaceans

Blackish underbelly is covered with light-producing photophores

Short gills on narrow, spindle-shaped body

GREENLAND SHARK

Somniosus microcephalus

The world's coldest oceans bring life into the slow lane. Beneath the Arctic ice, the Greenland shark is the slowest fish for its size and has a lazy taste for carrion (dead animals). Despite its sluggishness, this shark can be a crafty mover when it wants to be. It has even been known to grab reindeer that slip off the ice.

Small eye

DATA FILE

PREDATOR POWER

ⓘ ⓘ ⓘ ⓘ ⓘ

SIZE: Up to 23.9 ft (7.3 m) long

DISTRIBUTION: Cold, deep coastal waters of North Atlantic and Arctic oceans

DIET: Fish, invertebrates, seabirds, seals, and carrion

Greenland sharks may live for **more than 150 years.**

One of two small, similarly sized dorsal fins

This sluggish shark moves and breathes slowly, so has small gill slits

The pygmy shark's underbelly **glows in the dark.**

Narrow body tapers back toward tail

Pale marks on pectoral fins

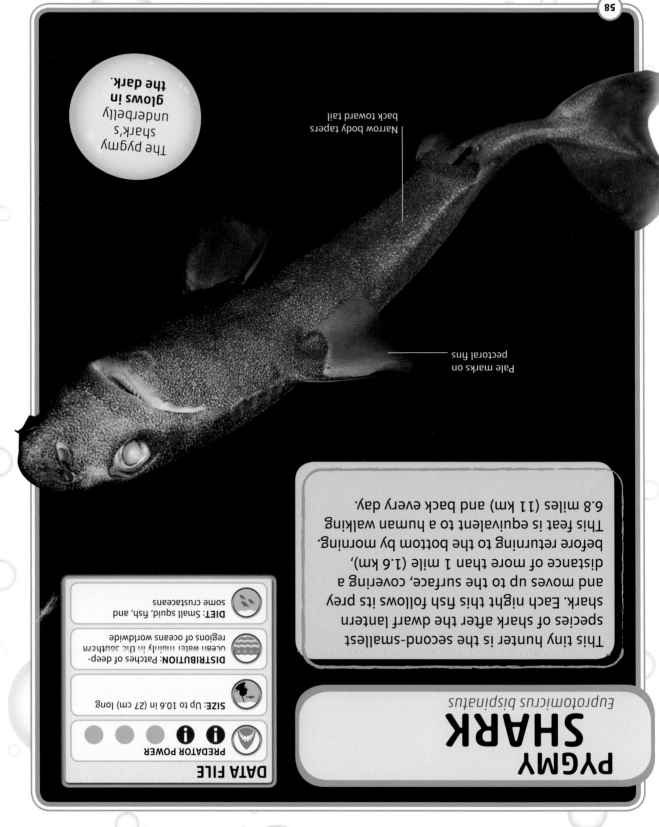

PYGMY SHARK
Euprotomicrus bispinatus

This tiny hunter is the second-smallest species of shark after the dwarf lantern shark. Each night this fish follows its prey and moves up to the surface, covering a distance of more than 1 mile (1.6 km), before returning to the bottom by morning. This feat is equivalent to a human walking 6.8 miles (11 km) and back every day.

DATA FILE

PREDATOR POWER

SIZE: Up to 10.6 in (27 cm) long

DISTRIBUTION: Patches of deep-ocean water mainly in the southern regions of oceans worldwide

DIET: Small squid, fish, and some crustaceans

COOKIECUTTER SHARK
Isistius brasiliensis

Although small, the cookiecutter is a terrifying carnivore. Bigger predators may approach the cookiecutter, just thinking it is easy prey. However, just as they try to bite, the cookiecutter strikes first. It clamps its razor-sharp teeth into its victim and twists around to remove a mouthful of meat.

Cookiecutter **bite marks** have been found on submarines.

Light-producing organs cover the underside of the body.

Dark collar on throat lacks light-producing organs.

DATA FILE

PREDATOR POWER

SIZE: Up to 19.7 in (50 cm) long

DISTRIBUTION: Deep-ocean waters worldwide

DIET: Grabs plugs of flesh from big fish and sometimes from dolphins, whales, and seals

SPINY DOGFISH
Squalus acanthias

The spiny dogfish might be called the piranha of the ocean. It moves in big shoals, and can use its jaws to cut bigger fish to pieces. It grows slowly and may live for more than 100 years—prowling the darkness of deep waters and sometimes coming further inshore.

Short spine at the front edge of each dorsal fin

KITEFIN SHARK
Dalatias licha

Like many deep-sea sharks, this hunter makes up for its moderate size with bold hunting tactics. The kitefin shark has heavy jaws and huge, serrated teeth, and uses them to lunge at bigger fish, tearing off chunks of flesh. Its oily liver keeps it buoyant, helping it to hover in mid-water as it waits to ambush prey that ventures too close.

Thick lips and powerful jaws

Large green eyes, like those in many other sharks found in deep, dark water

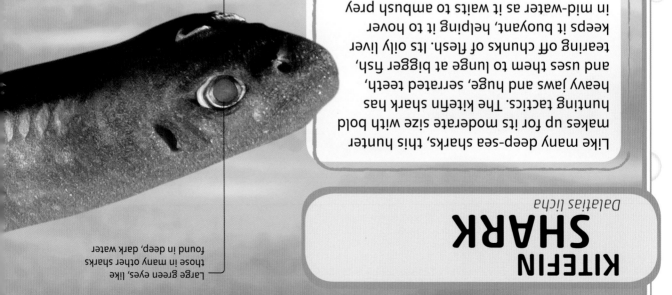

One of two widely separated, equal-sized dorsal fins

DATA FILE

PREDATOR POWER
❗ ❗ ❗ ❗ ❗

SIZE: Up to 5.9 ft (1.8 m) long

DISTRIBUTION: Deep waters of most parts of oceans worldwide and Mediterranean Sea

DIET: Fish (including other sharks), squid, crustaceans, and sometimes seals

This hunter may **attack** other, **bigger, sharks**.

The spiny dogfish may be the world's **most abundant** shark.

DATA FILE

PREDATOR POWER
❗ ❗ ○ ○ ○

SIZE: Up to 3.9 ft (1.2 m) long

DISTRIBUTION: Coastal waters of temperate oceans worldwide, and Mediterranean Sea

DIET: Other fish and invertebrates

Bluish-gray body, often with scattered white spots

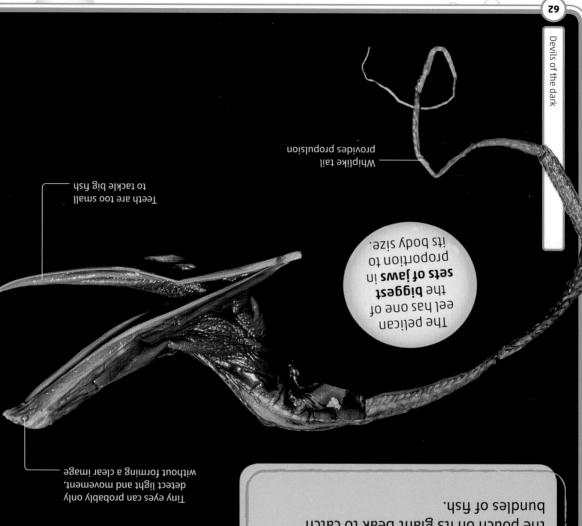

Whiplike tail
provides propulsion

Teeth are too small
to tackle big fish

The pelican
eel has one of
the **biggest
sets of jaws** in
proportion to
its body size.

Tiny eyes can probably only
detect light and movement,
without forming a clear image

PELICAN
EEL

Eurypharynx pelecanoides

The pelican eel's jaws are seven times
longer than its skull's brain case, and its
big mouth looks like it tackles giant prey.
However, the pelican eel probably uses
its enormous jaws to scoop up shoals of
shrimps, much like the pelican bird uses
the pouch on its giant beak to catch
bundles of fish.

DATA FILE

PREDATOR POWER

ⓘ ● ● ● ● ●

SIZE: Up to 3.3 ft (1 m) long

DISTRIBUTION: Deep waters of
oceans worldwide

DIET: Mainly small shrimps
and squid

SLADEN'S
HATCHETFISH
Argyropelecus sladeni

Upward-pointing mouth

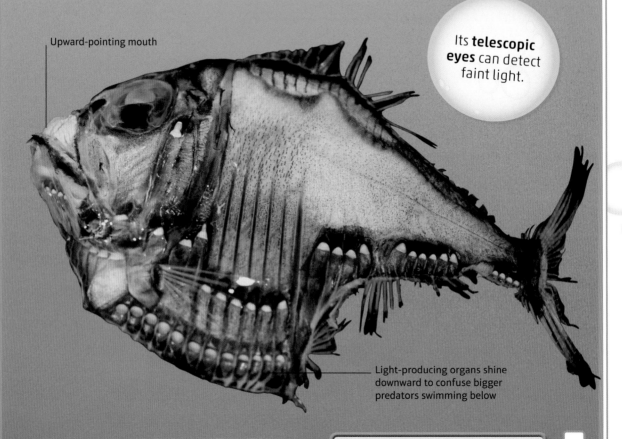

Its **telescopic eyes** can detect faint light.

Light-producing organs shine downward to confuse bigger predators swimming below

The tiny, deep-ocean hatchetfish uses clever tactics to be an effective ocean predator. Its bulging eyes are directed upward so they can spot the shadow of overhead plankton that are small enough to bite. Each night these fish migrate miles toward the surface to follow their prey.

DATA FILE

 PREDATOR POWER

 SIZE: Up to 2.8 in (7 cm) long

 DISTRIBUTION: Deep waters of oceans worldwide

 DIET: Copepods (small, swimming crustaceans)

Devils of the dark

BARBELED DRAGONFISH
Stomias boa

The barbeled dragonfish has light-producing organs running along its body, and its big scales reflect the light. It gets its name from the long, luminous barbel that projects from its chin—a feature that might help attract the attention of smaller fish, which are then grabbed by a mouth filled with long, pointed teeth.

Light produced by this fish **may confuse bigger predators**.

SLOANE'S VIPERFISH
Chauliodus sloani

When the viperfish attacks, its lower jaw reaches forward and the top of its head rotates backward. As a result, its mouth opens to nearly 180 degrees to take a bite. It strikes its victims with such force that it needs a specially adapted "neck" vertebrae to absorb the shock of the blow.

Viperfish, side view

"Fangs" are so long that it cannot completely close its jaws

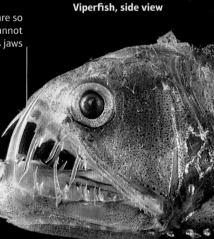

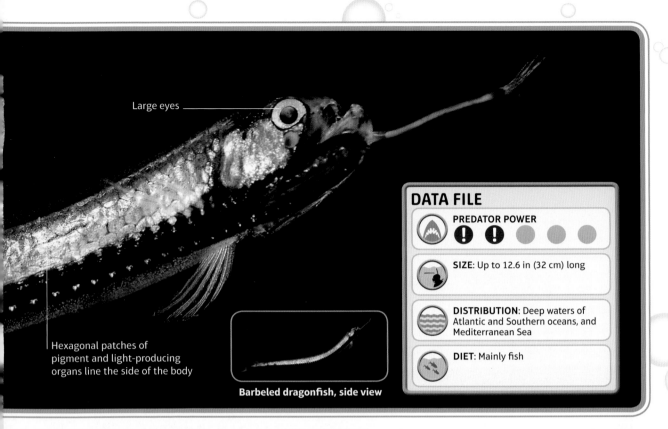

Large eyes

Hexagonal patches of
pigment and light-producing
organs line the side of the body

Barbeled dragonfish, side view

DATA FILE

PREDATOR POWER

SIZE: Up to 12.6 in (32 cm) long

DISTRIBUTION: Deep waters of
Atlantic and Southern oceans, and
Mediterranean Sea

DIET: Mainly fish

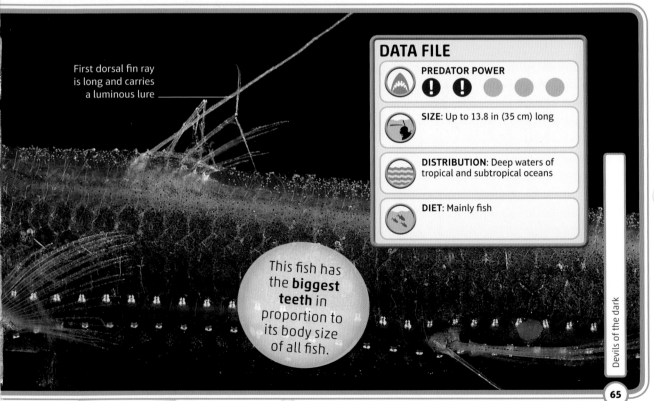

First dorsal fin ray
is long and carries
a luminous lure

This fish has
the **biggest
teeth** in
proportion to
its body size
of all fish.

DATA FILE

PREDATOR POWER

SIZE: Up to 13.8 in (35 cm) long

DISTRIBUTION: Deep waters of
tropical and subtropical oceans

DIET: Mainly fish

Devils of the dark

DEEP-SEA
LIZARDFISH
Bathysaurus ferox

The deep-sea lizardfish probably spends much of its time on the ocean bottom, rather than swimming in mid-water. Here it probably waits to ambush passing prey, making a grab with strong, alligator-like jaws that extend back beyond its black eyes. Its body is covered with a mosaic of tough scales, like a lizard's scaly skin.

The lizardfish's **barbed teeth** give it **a better grip** on prey.

Wide jaws with needlelike teeth may be strong enough to grab large prey

Skin covered in large, tough scales

Deep-sea lizardfish, top view

DATA FILE

 PREDATOR POWER

 SIZE: Up to 27.6 in (70 cm) long

 DISTRIBUTION: Deep waters of oceans worldwide

 DIET: Fish, squid, crabs, and dead animals drifting down from above

LANCETFISH

Alepisaurus sp.

Sail-like dorsal fin runs along the back of the body

Jaws contain two or three extra-large fangs among the smaller teeth

Lancetfish, side view

This has been called the **"cannibal fish"** because it **may eat its own kind**.

Although this fish resembles the speedy sailfish, it lacks the muscle power of that ocean athlete. The unrelated lancetfish relies instead on surprise to catch its prey, so prefers to hunt in deeper, darker water, grabbing anything it can gobble down. Its scientific name, *Alepisaurus*, means "lizard without scales"—a reference to its unusually smooth, somewhat flabby, skin.

DATA FILE

PREDATOR POWER

SIZE: Up to 6.9 ft (2.1 m) long

DISTRIBUTION: Deep waters of oceans worldwide

DIET: Fish, squid, and swimming crustaceans

Devils of the dark

HUMPBACK
ANGLERFISH
Melanocetus johnsonii

The humpback anglerfish has an extraordinary life history. Only females hunt by using a luminous lure to attract prey within reach of their massive jaws. Males are smaller, and those of some species of deep-sea angler never feed at all. Once a male finds his giant mate, he attaches to her and the pair spawn together.

GIANT
SQUID
Architeuthis dux

One of the world's biggest animals without a backbone is a little-known giant of the deep sea. Despite its enormous size, and tentacles that can reach longer than a bus, the giant squid is rarely seen. Once caught by the suckers on its tentacles, prey rarely escapes, and is quickly brought to the sharp beak to be dismembered.

Suckers on eight muscular arms and two tentacles help catch prey

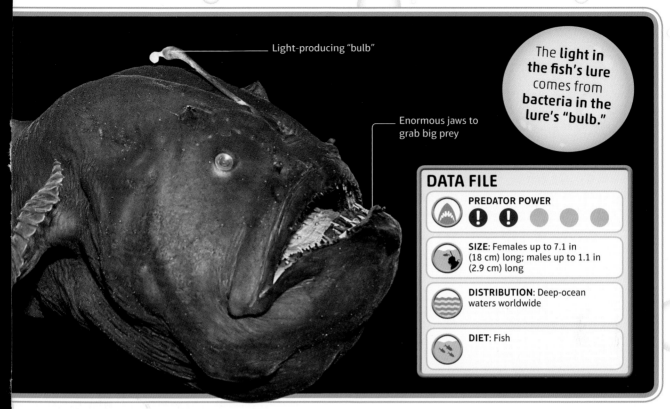

Light-producing "bulb"

Enormous jaws to
grab big prey

The **light in
the fish's lure**
comes from
**bacteria in the
lure's "bulb."**

DATA FILE

PREDATOR POWER
❗ ❗ ○ ○ ○

SIZE: Females up to 7.1 in
(18 cm) long; males up to 1.1 in
(2.9 cm) long

DISTRIBUTION: Deep-ocean
waters worldwide

DIET: Fish

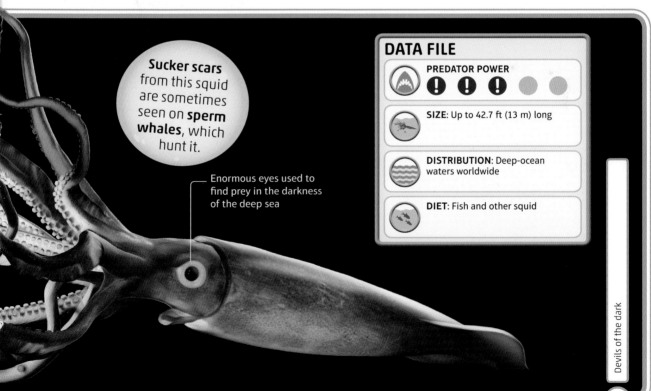

Sucker scars
from this squid
are sometimes
seen on **sperm
whales**, which
hunt it.

Enormous eyes used to
find prey in the darkness
of the deep sea

DATA FILE

PREDATOR POWER
❗ ❗ ❗ ○ ○

SIZE: Up to 42.7 ft (13 m) long

DISTRIBUTION: Deep-ocean
waters worldwide

DIET: Fish and other squid

Devils of the dark

VAMPIRE SQUID
Vampyroteuthis infernalis

The bizarre vampire squid is only distantly related to "true" squid. Among its unusual features are the threadlike "fishing lines" it uses rather than the tentacles usually found in squid. The vampire squid gets its name from its eyes, which sometimes seem to glow red. However, it is no blood-sucker, and instead preys on small, soft-bodied animals found in plankton.

Webbing connects the eight arms to form a "cloak"

Body covered in light-producing organs that can flash to confuse predators

When threatened, this creature gives off **blobs of blue, glowing mucus**.

DATA FILE

 PREDATOR POWER

SIZE: Up to 12 in (30 cm) long with arms extended

 DISTRIBUTION: Deep waters of oceans worldwide

 DIET: Planktonic animals, including small crustaceans and jellyfish

ZEBRA BULLHEAD

Heterodontus zebra

Bullhead sharks have very strong jaws for sharks of such small size. They grab crabs, snails, and urchins with sharp, pointed teeth at the front of the jaw and then smash the prey with blunter "cheek" teeth near the back. Many species have bold patterns, and the zebra bullhead is perhaps the most striking of them all.

Brownish, vertical stripes turn black as the shark matures

Cream-colored body

This fish is popular in **public aquariums**.

DATA FILE

 PREDATOR POWER

 SIZE: Up to 3.9 ft (1.2 m) long

 DISTRIBUTION: Shallow coastal waters of eastern Asia and north-western Australia

 DIET: Bottom-living invertebrates

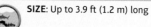

4

KILLERS BETWEEN THE TIDES

The coastline, where ocean meets land, is a challenging place to live. Each day the tides drain the shore of water and then flood it completely. However, many kinds of ocean animals can survive out of water during low tide, using rocks and seaweed for shelter. A few sharks even use their fins like legs to waddle between rock pools in search of stranded prey.

HORN
SHARK

Heterodontus francisci

The horn shark gets its name from the hornlike ridges over its eyes. It hunts for invertebrates along rocky shorelines, often using its muscular pectoral fins to clamber over the ocean bottom. Like other bullheads, the female horn shark lays spiral-shaped egg cases, wedging them between rocky crevices as extra protection from predators.

DATA FILE

 PREDATOR POWER

 SIZE: Up to 37.8 in (96 cm) long

 DISTRIBUTION: Shallow coastal waters of California, Mexico, and probably Ecuador and Peru

 DIET: Sea urchins, crabs, shrimps, worms, anemones, mollusks, and small fish

The horn shark has the **strongest bite** of any shark relative to its size.

Body has small, dark spots on a lighter background

Hornlike ridge

COLLARED CARPET SHARK

Parascyllium collare

DATA FILE

PREDATOR POWER

SIZE: Up to 34.2 in (87 cm) long

DISTRIBUTION: Shallow coastal waters of eastern Australia

DIET: Small, bottom-living fish and invertebrates

Small sharks that live in shallow water are vulnerable to bigger predators, but the markings of the collared carpet shark may help protect it. The markings allow this shark to disguise itself against the background of coral and seaweed. The fish may even alter its color to match the ocean floor.

Dark spots are scattered over most of the body

Paddle-like pectoral fin lacks spots

This shark lays **long egg cases**.

Like many other related sharks, this species has a dark collar marking the region of the gills

BLIND SHARK

Brachaelurus waddi

The blind shark looks more like a catfish than a shark. It hunts close to the shoreline, and can survive being out of water if stranded in low tide. This small, Australian predator has reasonable vision, but gets its name from its habit of closing its eyelids when danger threatens.

DATA FILE

 PREDATOR POWER

 SIZE: Up to 3.9 ft (1.2 m) long

 DISTRIBUTION: Seagrass or reefs of eastern Australia

 DIET: Sea anemones, squid, crustaceans, and small fish

One of two equal-sized dorsal fins

The blind shark can survive for **18 hours** out of water.

Small eye in front of extra-big spiracle, or respiratory opening

Long, sensory barbels help find prey

ORNATE
WOBBEGONG
Orectolobus ornatus

Wobbegongs are flat-bodied, bottom-living sharks that hunt at night. By day, they rely on the superb camouflage of their intricate color pattern to stay hidden. The ornate wobbegong likes to rest in underwater caves and under rocky ledges, sometimes in the safety of a large group. Humans that accidentally tread on a wobbegong may get seriously injured by their needlelike teeth.

DATA FILE

 PREDATOR POWER

 SIZE: Up to 3.6 ft (1.1 m) long

 DISTRIBUTION: Coral reefs and lagoons around New Guinea, and eastern and southern Australia

 DIET: Fish (including other sharks), squid, octopuses, and crustaceans

Colored patches have white spots and crinkled edges

This wobbegong uses its pectoral fins to **"walk"** over rocks.

SPOTTED WOBBEGONG

Orectolobus maculatus

Like other wobbegongs, the spotted wobbegong may be seen on the shoreline in shallow water barely deep enough to cover its body. It can even use its strong, flexible pectoral fins like big feet for clambering over rocks from one tidal pool to another. It rests in caves and shipwrecks during the day.

Sharks of this species are known to **rest together, piled up in groups**.

Patchy color pattern camouflages the shark against the seabed

DATA FILE

 PREDATOR POWER

 SIZE: Up to 5.6 ft (1.7 m) long

 DISTRIBUTION: Coral reefs and seagrass around Australia

 DIET: Fish (including other sharks), crabs, lobsters, and octopuses

Killers between the tides

COBBLER
WOBBEGONG
Sutorectus tentaculatus

The cobbler wobbegong's body is not as broad and flat as that of other wobbegongs, but it is just as well camouflaged against the Australian sea floor. Its intricate pattern of jigsaw-like skin markings looks so much like the seabed that it is easily overlooked by divers, so little is known about its life.

DATA FILE

 PREDATOR POWER

 SIZE: Up to 36.2 in (92 cm) long

 DISTRIBUTION: Coral reefs of western and southern Australia

 DIET: Bony fish and invertebrates

Cobbler wobbegong, side view

Colored patterns with jagged-edged streaks

TASSELLED
WOBBEGONG
Eucrossorhinus dasypogon

Of all the strange, bottom-living wobbegongs, the tasselled wobbegong has the best camouflage of them all. Its elaborate tassels look just like fronds of seaweed. This helps it blend well into the coral reef background. With such a perfect disguise, this fish can afford to swim quite slowly, although it can lunge with lightning speed to catch prey with its enormous mouth.

This shark can grab prey in a **fraction of a second**.

Complicated pattern of lines and spots

"Beard" of branching tassels

DATA FILE

 PREDATOR POWER

 SIZE: Up to 4.2 ft (1.3 m) long

 DISTRIBUTION: Coral reefs of Southeast Asia, New Guinea, and northern Australia

 DIET: Bottom-living fish and, possibly, invertebrates

EPAULETTE
SHARK
Hemiscyllium ocellatum

The epaulette shark can survive remarkably well out of water, among moist, rocky crevices. It is often found in tidal pools, where low tides might leave the fish entirely exposed. When disturbed, it hides by burying its head in coral and seaweed, while the rest of its body stays completely visible.

Strong, flexible pectoral and pelvic fins help the shark clamber over rocks

Epaulette shark, front view

GIANT PACIFIC
OCTOPUS
Enteroctopus dofleini

This octopus can **weigh** as much as **600 lb (272 kg)**.

Eye has a horizontal pupil

Like other octopuses, this species can change color by expanding tiny sacs of pigment in its skin

Double row of suckers on each of the eight arms grips prey tightly

The giant Pacific octopus grows bigger and lives longer than any other octopus species. An adult female giant Pacific octopus can produce up to 100,000 eggs. A devoted mother, she guards her eggs for five to eight months before they hatch. She also stops hunting, becoming so weak that she dies soon after the eggs hatch.

DATA FILE

 PREDATOR POWER

 SIZE: Arm span of up to 31.5 ft (9.6 m)

 DISTRIBUTION: Coastal and deep waters of North Pacific Ocean

 DIET: Shrimps, crabs, lobsters, clams, scallops, abalones, and fish (including small sharks)

Devils of the dark

White-edged, black shoulder spot looks like the ornamental epaulette of a military uniform

This shark can **survive for hours out of water** without breathing.

DATA FILE

PREDATOR POWER
❗ ❗ ⬤ ⬤ ⬤

SIZE: Up to 3.6 ft (1.1 m) long

DISTRIBUTION: Coral reefs of New Guinea, and northern and eastern Australia

DIET: Mainly worms, crabs, and shrimps

Killers between the tides

WHITE-SPOTTED
BAMBOOSHARK
Chiloscyllium plagiosum

White spots scattered over body

The bambooshark's small, slender body helps it to get between rocky crevices and among coral, either to find shelter from danger or to locate prey. If they get stranded by an ebbing tide, they do not have to worry—some can survive out of water for half a day.

VENUS
COMB
Murex pecten

Not all snails are harmless herbivores. Members of the whelk family, such as this one, prey on other invertebrates. The Venus comb uses a muscular foot to bore into the shells of other mollusks and barnacles. It then eats the flesh using an extendable body part called a proboscis. The Venus comb gets its name because its shell resembles a hair comb.

This shark lays **up to 26 egg cases** per season.

One of two dorsal fins set far back on long tail

DATA FILE

PREDATOR POWER

SIZE: Up to 37.4 in (95 cm) long

DISTRIBUTION: Coral reefs around India, Southeast Asia, and Japan

DIET: Fish and crustaceans

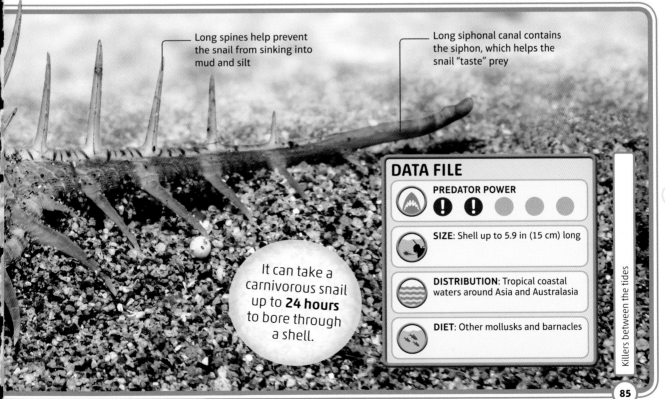

Long spines help prevent the snail from sinking into mud and silt

Long siphonal canal contains the siphon, which helps the snail "taste" prey

It can take a carnivorous snail up to **24 hours** to bore through a shell.

DATA FILE

PREDATOR POWER

SIZE: Shell up to 5.9 in (15 cm) long

DISTRIBUTION: Tropical coastal waters around Asia and Australasia

DIET: Other mollusks and barnacles

CONE
SHELL
Conus sp.

Many shell collectors have been badly stung by a cone shell. Its venom is the most potent produced by any kind of snail, and rivals the effects of the ocean's most venomous creatures. The cone shell delivers the venom by projecting a muscular body part called a proboscis, at the tip of which is a rapid-release harpoon that stabs the flesh of the victim.

DATA FILE

 PREDATOR POWER
! ! ! ! ●

 SIZE: Shell up to 9.1 in (23 cm) long, depending upon species

 DISTRIBUTION: Tropical coastal ocean waters worldwide

 DIET: Fish, worms, and other mollusks

Siphon channels seawater into the snail so it can "taste" the presence of prey

Single, muscular creeping foot helps cone shell glide along

Brightly colored,
cone-shaped shell

A cone shell **takes just minutes** to kill and swallow a fish.

COMMON STARFISH
Asterias rubens

Starfish may look harmless, but they are really slow-moving predators. They crawl on hundreds of fleshy "tube feet," so need to target similarly sluggish prey. A hungry starfish pulls on the shell halves of a mussel until the mollusk is weakened and a gap appears. Then the starfish sticks its stomach through the gap and digests the mussel while it is still alive.

DATA FILE

PREDATOR POWER

SIZE: Arm span of up to 12 in (30 cm)

DISTRIBUTION: Coastal waters of North Atlantic Ocean

DIET: Mollusks and other slow, bottom-living invertebrates

Each arm can be regenerated if it is lost

Hundreds of tiny tube feet

A starfish can **take up to two hours** to pull apart the shells of a mussel.

SOUTHERN BLUE-RINGED
OCTOPUS
Hapalochlaena maculosa

A bite from a blue-ringed octopus could **kill a human in 20 minutes**.

Electric-blue rings

Brown bands along the arms darken when the octopus gets agitated

Octopuses are intelligent hunters. There are many kinds that use bulk and strength to overpower prey, but the tiny blue-ringed octopus uses a powerful venom instead. Its startling electric-blue pattern serves as a warning for bigger animals to stay away. A single bite from this hunter could be fatal for a human.

DATA FILE

PREDATOR POWER

SIZE: Arm span of up to 7.9 in (20 cm)

DISTRIBUTION: Coastal ocean waters off southern Australia

DIET: Mainly crustaceans and bivalve mollusks, but sometimes fish

Killers between the tides

5
MUSCLE-MOUTHED GULPERS

Some sea-living predators have such a large mouth that prey just gets sucked inside. These kinds of hunters can afford to lead a more sedate lifestyle than the ones that are speedy enough to lunge. Some even wait motionless for prey to come close, until it's gone in a single, sudden gulp.

WHALE SHARK

Rhincodon typus

The real giant among sharks grazes gently on plankton, small fish, and squid. The whale shark cruises the sunlit, upper ocean with its enormous mouth open wide to suck in water. Special pads at the back of this shark's mouth strain out tiny animals from the water. The whale shark then swallows these animals down a food pipe that is no wider than a man's arm.

Unique, checkerboard pattern of white spots on gray body

Rough skin, up to 6 in (15 cm) thick in places, is thicker than that of any other animal

Small eyes on either side of the enormous mouth

DATA FILE

PREDATOR POWER

SIZE: Up to 65.6 ft (20 m) long

DISTRIBUTION: Surface waters of tropical and warm temperate oceans worldwide

DIET: Plankton (including krill), small fish, and squid

Muscle-mouthed gulpers

Wide mouth for collecting prey

The whale shark is the **world's biggest living fish**.

ZEBRA SHARK
Stegostoma fasciatum

The zebra shark is a typical suction-feeder, and it captures prey hidden in the sand by sucking it up like a vacuum cleaner. When scientists first studied young zebra sharks, they thought the fish would keep their stripes. That is how these sharks got their name. However, as they grow bigger, their stripes are replaced by spots.

DATA FILE

 PREDATOR POWER

 SIZE: Up to 7.9 ft (2.4 m) long

 DISTRIBUTION: Shallow coastal waters of tropical Indian and western Pacific oceans

 DIET: Mainly mollusks, shrimps, crabs, and small fish

Newborn zebra sharks may **mimic** the appearance of venomous **sea snakes**.

Leopard-like, spotted pattern

Large spiracle (respiratory opening)

NURSE SHARK

Ginglymostoma cirratum

This shark can **suck big snails** out of their shells.

The nurse shark could be the strongest suction-feeding shark of all. By rapidly expanding its throat cavity, it can swallow prey faster than any other shark. When it does this, it makes a slurping sound like a nursing baby, which may be the source of its name.

The mouth looks small, but has very strong suction

Sensory barbels help the shark find prey

Strong pectoral fins often help shark to walk on the seabed

Nurse shark, side view

DATA FILE

 PREDATOR POWER
❗ ❗ ⬤ ⬤ ⬤

SIZE: Up to 9.8 ft (3 m) long

DISTRIBUTION: Shallow coastal waters of tropical Atlantic and eastern Pacific oceans, and Caribbean Sea

DIET: Bottom-dwelling invertebrates, bony fish, and sting rays

Muscle-mouthed gulpers

TAWNY
NURSE SHARK
Nebrius ferrugineus

This suction-feeder hunts mainly at night, spending the day in the shelter of caves, where several resting sharks may be piled on top of one another. When hunting, the tawny nurse shark can suck fish from between rocks. When caught by anglers, it can spit water in the face of its captor.

Snout is wedge-shaped, with two barbels on the under surface

ANGLERFISH
Lophius piscatorius

The deep-sea anglerfish is a superbly camouflaged seabed predator that has a lure for attracting prey. It waves a little flag on the front of its head, just above its mouth, to attract the attention of a hungry, passing fish. It then uses extendable jaws to snatch its victim in a rapid-action reflex.

Paddle-like pelvic and pectoral fins help the fish "walk" on the ocean floor

Muscle-mouthed gulpers

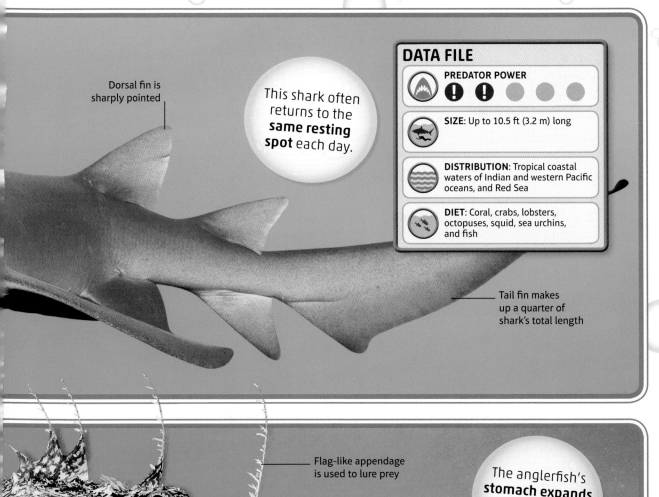

Dorsal fin is
sharply pointed

This shark often
returns to the
**same resting
spot** each day.

DATA FILE

PREDATOR POWER
! !

SIZE: Up to 10.5 ft (3.2 m) long

DISTRIBUTION: Tropical coastal
waters of Indian and western Pacific
oceans, and Red Sea

DIET: Coral, crabs, lobsters,
octopuses, squid, sea urchins,
and fish

Tail fin makes
up a quarter of
shark's total length

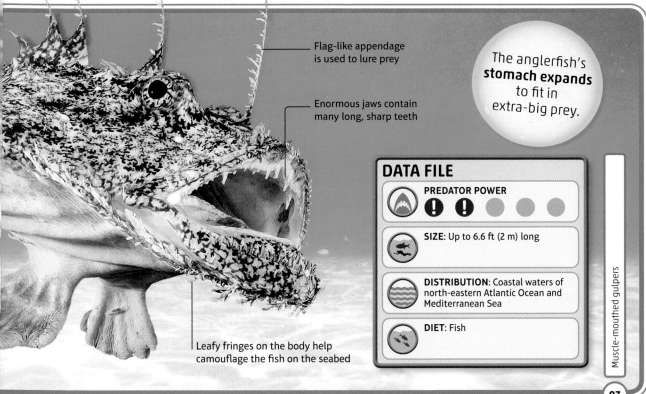

Flag-like appendage
is used to lure prey

Enormous jaws contain
many long, sharp teeth

The anglerfish's
stomach expands
to fit in
extra-big prey.

Leafy fringes on the body help
camouflage the fish on the seabed

DATA FILE

PREDATOR POWER
! !

SIZE: Up to 6.6 ft (2 m) long

DISTRIBUTION: Coastal waters of
north-eastern Atlantic Ocean and
Mediterranean Sea

DIET: Fish

Muscle-mouthed gulpers

PSYCHEDELIC FROGFISH
Histiophryne psychedelica

Frogfish are the most impressive of the walking anglerfish, having strongly angled fins that serve as feet for waddling along the ocean floor. It lacks the long lure that other anglerfish use to attract prey, and instead relies on its remarkable pattern to blend in with the coral-reef background while waiting to ambush prey.

DATA FILE

 PREDATOR POWER

 SIZE: Up to 5.9 in (15 cm) long

 DISTRIBUTION: Tropical coastal waters around islands of Bali and the Moluccas in Indonesia

 DIET: Shrimps and small fish

Exact pattern of white, swirling stripes is unique to each individual

The frilly cheeks may **detect the movement** of predators or prey.

Crawling pectoral fins look like limbs of frogs

Muscle-mouthed gulpers

PINK FROGMOUTH
Chaunax pictus

PREDATOR POWER
! !

SIZE: Up to 15.7 in (40 cm) long

DISTRIBUTION: Tropical coastal waters of Atlantic Ocean and Mediterranean Sea

DIET: Fish and invertebrates

For ocean predators that are not athletic swimmers, the best tactic is to lie in wait and ambush prey. This balloon-bodied predator belongs to a group of wide-mouthed anglerfish that have sometimes been called sea toads. The pink frogmouth has a lure to attract prey, but also has fleshy fins for "walking" on the ocean floor.

Tiny, spinelike scales make this fish's body surface rough.

Short, wiggling lure attracts prey

Squat, leglike pectoral fins

Golden spots on pink skin

Muscle-mouthed gulpers

GIANT GROUPER

Epinephelus lanceolatus

This enormous fish is one of the top predators—and biggest bony fish—of the tropical reef. It has a voracious appetite and will eat anything that can fit into its mouth, even small sharks. The biggest individuals live out their mostly solitary lives around the vicinity of an underwater cave that is their "lair."

DATA FILE

 PREDATOR POWER

 SIZE: Up to 8.9 ft (2.7 m) long

 DISTRIBUTION: Tropical coastal waters of Indian and western Pacific oceans

DIET: Mainly crustaceans, but also fish and young sea turtles

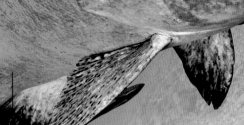

Huge fleshy-lipped mouth sucks in prey

Bright patches of color on juvenile turn dull gray as the fish grows older

Giant groupers **change from female to male** as they mature.

STONEFISH
Synanceia verrucosa

Stonefish have one of the **deadliest venoms** of **all fish**.

Changeable color pattern provides perfect camouflage against rocky rubble

Wide, upturned mouth gulps prey swimming overhead

Stonefish, side view

The stonefish is a master of camouflage. This big-mouthed predator stays so perfectly disguised among rocks and coral that an unwary snorkeler could easily tread on its venomous spines, resulting in agonizing pain. The fish can survive in the shallowest water in the intertidal zone.

DATA FILE

PREDATOR POWER

SIZE: Up to 15.7 in (40 cm) long

DISTRIBUTION: Tropical coastal waters of Indian and western Pacific oceans, and Red Sea

DIET: Fish and crustaceans

Muscle-mouthed gulpers

COMMON
LIONFISH
Pterois miles

The enormous mouth of this striking predator can suck in all sorts of prey, while its highly venomous spines protect it from practically any large hunter. The common lionfish has a voracious appetite and can reproduce at an astonishing rate, too. This means it can overrun and damage reef habitats in which it has been introduced.

Venomous spines used in self-defense

When flared outward, pectoral fins help bunch prey into tighter groups

DATA FILE

PREDATOR POWER

SIZE: Up to 13.8 in (35 cm) long

DISTRIBUTION: Tropical coastal waters of Indian Ocean and Red Sea

DIET: Fish and invertebrates

Muscle-mouthed gulpers

This predator's stomach can grow **30 times larger** when filling up with prey.

Large, shovel-shaped mouth can swallow big prey

Stripy pattern helps break up the outline of the lionfish

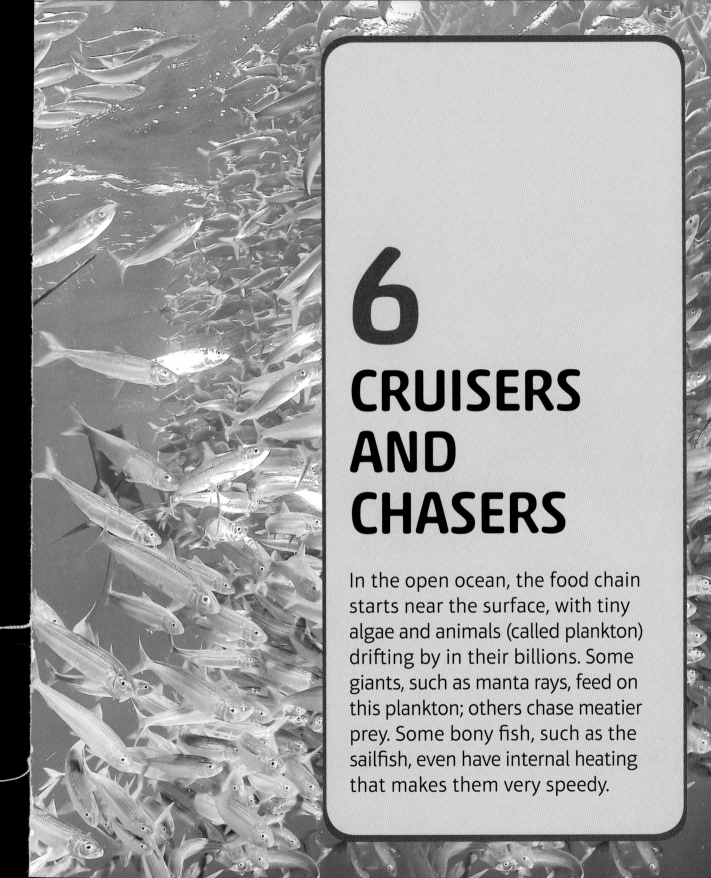

6
CRUISERS AND CHASERS

In the open ocean, the food chain starts near the surface, with tiny algae and animals (called plankton) drifting by in their billions. Some giants, such as manta rays, feed on this plankton; others chase meatier prey. Some bony fish, such as the sailfish, even have internal heating that makes them very speedy.

BASKING SHARK

Cetorhinus maximus

The basking shark has a sedate lifestyle. This giant cruises the ocean's waters with its mouth gaping to filter planktonic food. Unlike the bigger whale shark, this fish does not gulp water, but takes in water like a giant funnel; enough to fill two Olympic-sized swimming pools every hour.

Enormous gill slits almost completely encircle the head

The largest basking sharks can **weigh over 3 tons**.

DATA FILE

 PREDATOR POWER

 SIZE: Up to 33 ft (10 m) long

 DISTRIBUTION: Oceans worldwide outside the tropics, and Mediterranean Sea

 DIET: Shrimps, fish eggs, small fish, and other planktonic animals

Small eyes at the base of conical snout

Cavernous mouth funnels plankton-rich water over the gills

MEGAMOUTH SHARK

Megachasma pelagios

When scientists found the first megamouth shark in 1976, they decided it was unusual and classified it in a new family on its own. This giant is a filter-feeder and a slow swimmer, but it makes up for it by an impressive vertical migration. It follows plankton into deep waters by day, and rises to the surface at night.

DATA FILE

  PREDATOR POWER

 SIZE: Up to 18 ft (5.5 m) long

 DISTRIBUTION: Found in patches of open ocean worldwide

 DIET: Mainly shrimps of the ocean's plankton, small fish, and jellyfish

There have been only about **60 sightings** of the megamouth.

Flabby body contains an oil-rich liver that makes the fish more buoyant in water

Megamouth shark, side view

Wide mouth opens to funnel seawater over the gills, where plankton is filtered out and swallowed

SMALL-TOOTHED
SANDTIGER SHARK

Odontaspis ferox

Although the small-toothed sandtiger often swims in open water over the deep ocean, it regularly patrols rocky reefs, drop-offs, and gullies. Like its close relatives, it is an active hunter. This shark has slightly bigger eyes than the sandtiger shark, suggesting it is more used to searching for prey in darker waters.

Grayish body helps to distinguish this shark from the browner sandtiger shark

Long teeth give the mouth a "toothy" appearance

DATA FILE

PREDATOR POWER

SIZE: Up to 14.7 ft (4.5 m) long

DISTRIBUTION: Coastal and deep waters of oceans worldwide and Mediterranean Sea

DIET: Fish, squid, and shrimps

This shark is also known as the **bumpytail ragged-tooth**.

Cruisers and chasers

109

SANDTIGER
SHARK

Carcharias taurus

Slightly flattened, conical snout

Long, slender teeth give the shark a "toothy" appearance

The sandtiger shark **gulps air** for extra **buoyancy**.

The sandtiger shark has one of the biggest brains of related shark species, making it a clever hunter. Groups of sandtiger shark may work together to "herd" shoals of fish, often coming near coastlines and over reefs to do so. These predators have a complex courtship too, and males even guard females after mating.

DATA FILE

 PREDATOR POWER
❗ ❗ ❗ ⬤ ⬤

 SIZE: Up to 10.5 ft (3.2 m) long

 DISTRIBUTION: Coastal waters of warm, temperate and tropical oceans, and Mediterranean Sea

 DIET: Fish and invertebrates

CROCODILE SHARK
Pseudocarcharias kamoharai

Crocodile sharks may **migrate to the surface** at night, perhaps trailing prey.

Large eyes

Like most sharks, lower jaw projects forward (is "extensible") to help shark grab prey easily

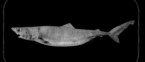

Crocodile shark, side view

This small, swift-moving hunter spends its days in deep water, so is rarely seen. The crocodile shark uses its big eyes to hunt in near darkness. Like some other related sharks, it has a small litter size, but stronger youngsters may eat their weaker siblings while they are still inside their mother's womb.

DATA FILE

PREDATOR POWER
 ❗ ❗ ❗ ● ●

 SIZE: Up to 3.9 ft (1.2 m) long

 DISTRIBUTION: Deep ocean waters of tropical oceans worldwide

 DIET: Fish, squid, and shrimps

GREAT
WHITE SHARK
Carcharodon carcharias

The great white shark probably has the strongest bite of any living animal. It usually lives in the upper layers of the open ocean, but often comes near the shore in search of prey. Younger great whites hunt for fish. As these sharks grow bigger, they turn to more warm-blooded prey, and are drawn to places where seals are abundant along the shoreline.

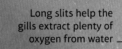

Long slits help the gills extract plenty of oxygen from water

Great whites can detect a **drop of blood** from **3 miles (5 km) away**.

Great white shark, side view

Massive, strong jaws
can easily grab ocean
mammals, such as seals
and large fish

White underside
contrasts sharply
with gray upper body

DATA FILE

PREDATOR POWER
! ! ! ! !

SIZE: Up to 19.7 ft (6 m) long

DISTRIBUTION: Open coastal
waters in oceans worldwide

DIET: Seals, dolphins, turtles,
seabirds, and large fish

Cruisers and chasers

SHORT-FINNED
MAKO
Isurus oxyrinchus

Blue or purplish color helps disguise the mako shark against the background of the open ocean

Streamlined shape helps this shark move faster in the water

A mako is known to have covered **8,077 miles (13,000 km)** in six months.

The muscular mako shark shoots through water in bursts of speed that can reach 60 mph (100 kph), making it a champion hunter of the open ocean and the fastest shark of all. Sometimes mako sharks will even jump right out of the water. They make extraordinary migrations too, crossing huge stretches of ocean at a time.

DATA FILE

 PREDATOR POWER

SIZE: Up to 13.1 ft (4 m) long

DISTRIBUTION: Open and coastal waters of oceans worldwide and Mediterranean Sea

 DIET: Mainly fish and squid; larger sharks hunt small dolphins

Cruisers and chasers

SALMON SHARK

Lamna ditropis

The high body temperature of this warm-blooded shark helps it stay active even when it is in cold water. This means its range can extend right into the chilly extremes of the far northern Pacific, where it can keep hunting in water too cold for many other sharks. The salmon shark hunts in groups to chase schools of fish, following the migrations of prey.

PREDATOR POWER

SIZE: Up to 9.8 ft (3 m) long

DISTRIBUTION: Open and coastal waters of North Pacific Ocean

DIET: Schooling fish, such as salmon and herrings

This shark is known to **hunt in groups** of 30 or 40.

Dusky blotches on paler underside of body

Long gill slits help the shark get plenty of oxygen from water

Cruisers and chasers

THRESHER SHARK

Alopias vulpinus

Few ocean animals can match the athleticism of the thresher shark. It chases prey just below the surface of the open ocean and has an astonishing technique for subduing targets. It uses the strap-like upper lobe of its tail, which grows the length of its body, to whip the water, stunning small fish so they can be easily gobbled up.

DATA FILE

 PREDATOR POWER
❗ ❗ ❗ ● ●

 SIZE: Up to 19 ft (5.8 m)

 DISTRIBUTION: Coastal and open-ocean waters worldwide

 DIET: Small fish, such as anchovies and mackerel, and squid, octopuses, and crustaceans

Extra-long upper lobe of tail

White patch extending above the pectoral fin identifies this species from other threshers

The **speed of this shark's tail** whip can be up to **80.7 mph (130 kph)**.

Narrow, sickle-shaped pectoral fins

GOBLIN SHARK

Mitsukurina owstoni

Long, flat snout packed with sensors that detect prey

Small eyes suggest vision is poor

A soft body suggests the goblin shark **swims mid-water**.

Nail-like teeth

Goblin shark, side view

Flabby skin

One of the most bizarre of all sharks, the goblin shark is a ghostly pale pink. Its body is so soft and flabby that it is probably not a strong swimmer. To find prey, it sweeps the water with its long, sensitive snout. Then it shoots out extensible jaws to snap at any prey within reach.

DATA FILE

 PREDATOR POWER

SIZE: Up to 12.5 ft (3.8 m) long

DISTRIBUTION: Open oceans worldwide

  DIET: Probably deep-water, soft-bodied fish and squid

SPOTTED EAGLE RAY
Aetobatus narinari

Tail may have 2–6 venomous spines

Enormous pectoral fins flap to make the ray "fly" through water

Eagle rays often **perform acrobatics** by jumping out of the water.

Shovel-like lower jaw digs for prey in sand

This close relative of the manta ray shares its cousin's habit of swimming in open water. However, unlike the manta, the spotted eagle ray does not feed on plankton. Instead, it hunts for bottom-living prey. Its strong jaws can crunch through a crab's hard shell.

DATA FILE

 PREDATOR POWER

 SIZE: Up to 16.4 ft (5 m) long and 10.8 ft (3.3 m) wide

DISTRIBUTION: Tropical coastal waters of western Atlantic, Indian, and Pacific oceans

 DIET: Mollusks, crabs, octopuses, small fish, and worms

GIANT MANTA RAY
Manta birostris

This giant among rays cruises the open ocean with graceful flaps of its "wings." Unlike most other rays, which are bottom-living, the manta ray is a swimming filter-feeder. It funnels plankton-rich water into its enormous mouth with the help of its hornlike cephalic fins. Special spongy structures on its gills then strain out the food.

Giant manta ray, top view

Hornlike cephalic fins curve around to funnel plankton-rich water into mouth

DATA FILE

 PREDATOR POWER
❗ ● ● ● ●

 SIZE: Up to 14.8 ft (4.5 m) long and 29.5 ft (9 m) wide

DISTRIBUTION: Tropical and subtropical open-ocean waters worldwide

 DIET: Shrimps, krill, and other small planktonic animals

The giant manta ray is the **world's biggest species of ray**.

GREAT
BARRACUDA
Sphyraena barracuda

Barracudas have long, pointed jaws and fang-like teeth that are not only perfect for grabbing small prey, but also good for ripping off lumps of flesh from bigger animals. Smaller barracudas hunt together in shoals in the open ocean, but the biggest ones live alone and have even been known to injure human divers.

DATA FILE

 PREDATOR POWER

 SIZE: Up to at least 6.6 ft (2 m) long

 DISTRIBUTION: Tropical and subtropical open ocean worldwide

 DIET: Fish, cephalopods, and occasionally shrimps

One of two widely separated dorsal fins

Pike-like jaws and daggerlike teeth

Barracudas can attack with bursts of **speed up to 36 mph (58 kph)**.

SAILFISH
Istiophorus albicans

Long, swordlike bill

Sail is raised to scare prey into tighter shoals, but lowered for high-speed chases

A fast-moving hunter of the open ocean, the sailfish is perfectly equipped for high-speed chases. As well as having a streamlined body that can cut through water easily, it stores extra oxygen in its red muscles. It can even generate heat in its head, which helps it keep its brain and eyes working efficiently.

DATA FILE

PREDATOR POWER
 ! !

SIZE: Up to 10.5 ft (3.2 m) long

DISTRIBUTION: Tropical and subtropical open ocean worldwide

DIET: Fish and squid

The sailfish is the **world's fastest** fish. It can reach speeds up to 68 mph (110 kph).

ATLANTIC
BLUEFIN TUNA
Thunnus thynnus

Tuna can swim at **speeds of 45 mph (72.4 kph)**.

Bright yellow "finlets" between second dorsal fin and tail

Metallic blue above, silver white below

The Atlantic bluefin tuna generates more body heat than almost any other kind of fish. This trait, along with the high oxygen-carrying capacity of its blood, makes it one of the speediest athletes in the ocean. The power for swimming comes from its flicking tail, while its body stays rigid to create a sleeker shape that cuts through the water with ease.

DATA FILE

 PREDATOR POWER ❗ ❗

 SIZE: Up to 15.1 ft (4.6 m) long

 DISTRIBUTION: Open waters of Atlantic Ocean and Mediterranean Sea

 DIET: Squid, fish, and crustaceans

GIANT TREVALLY
Caranx ignobilis

DATA FILE

 PREDATOR POWER

 SIZE: Up to 5.6 ft (1.7 m) long

 DISTRIBUTION: Tropical and subtropical coastal waters of Indian and Pacific oceans, and Red Sea

 DIET: Fish, squid, and crustaceans

This fish belongs to a family that is related to the sailfish and other open-ocean athletes, but the giant trevally sticks closer to coastal reefs. Juveniles even enter rivers and estuaries. The fish hunts alone or in groups. Individuals sometimes ambush their prey by hiding in the cover of big sharks.

This fish sometimes follows hunting seals to **steal their prey**.

Prominent, high forehead

Keels along the side of the body help increase swimming speed

Cruisers and chasers

HUMPBACK
WHALE
Megaptera novaeangliae

Particularly long pectoral flippers help make this species the most acrobatic of giant whales

The humpback's song is the **loudest and most complex** of any whale.

Despite its size, the humpback whale is one of the most agile of whale species. Its giant flippers are bigger than those of any other animal, and help it make sharp turns in the water for bunching shoals of fish and shrimps. It even blows a screen of bubbles from its blowhole to prevent their escape.

Grooves and elasticated skin allow expansion of throat to take in a huge volume of water containing prey

DATA FILE

PREDATOR POWER

SIZE: Up to 39 ft (11.9 m) long

DISTRIBUTION: Open ocean worldwide

DIET: Small fish and krill

SPERM
WHALE
Physeter macrocephalus

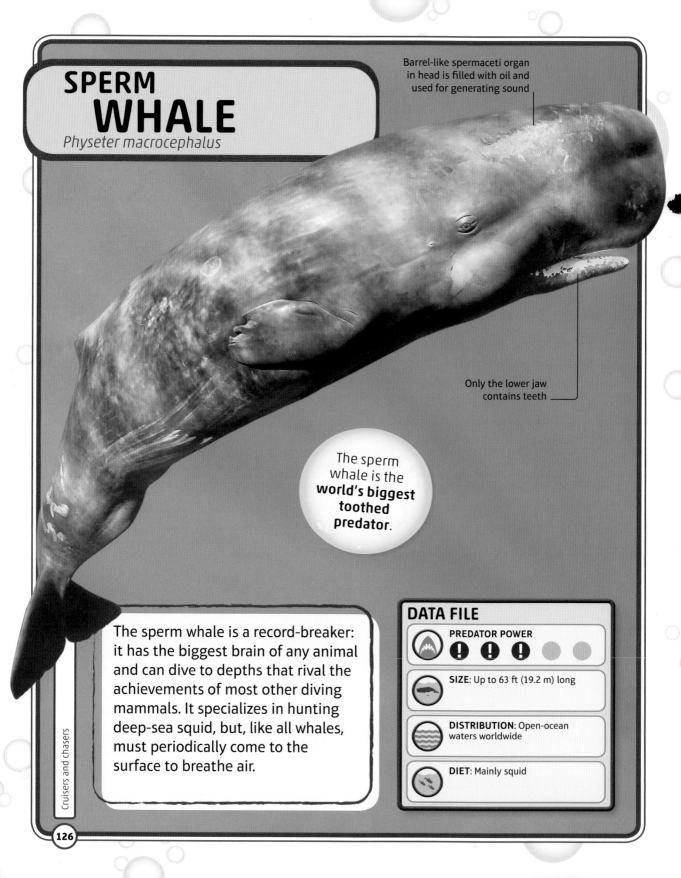

Barrel-like spermaceti organ in head is filled with oil and used for generating sound

Only the lower jaw contains teeth

The sperm whale is the **world's biggest toothed predator**.

The sperm whale is a record-breaker: it has the biggest brain of any animal and can dive to depths that rival the achievements of most other diving mammals. It specializes in hunting deep-sea squid, but, like all whales, must periodically come to the surface to breathe air.

DATA FILE

PREDATOR POWER
! ! !

SIZE: Up to 63 ft (19.2 m) long

DISTRIBUTION: Open-ocean waters worldwide

DIET: Mainly squid

Cruisers and chasers

LEATHERBACK
TURLE
Dermochelys coriacea

The leatherback turtle can travel more than 37.3 miles (60 km) in a day, with scarcely any rest during this time. Most reptiles are cold-blooded, so they are not very active in cold conditions, but this turtle can generate so much body heat it can even keep hunting in cold waters approaching the Arctic Circle.

This is the world's **biggest species of turtle**.

Leathery skin instead of hard-plated shell

Enormous flippers make this turtle a powerful swimmer

DATA FILE

PREDATOR POWER
❗ ❗ ⦿ ⦿ ⦿

SIZE: Usually up to 5.9 ft (1.8 m) long

DISTRIBUTION: Open-ocean waters worldwide

DIET: Almost entirely jellyfish, but sometimes squid and other soft-bodied animals

Cruisers and chasers

BOX JELLYFISH

Chironex sp.

Human swimmers fear the box jellyfish more than any other because of its terrible sting. Large swarms may gather during warmer months, often near the shore. This creature uses eyes to help find food. Its long tentacles can catch fish, paralysing them with powerful venom.

Cube-shaped bell

Long tentacles have thousands of stingers

Unlike other jellyfish, this one's **bell has eyes** to sense light and movement.

DATA FILE

PREDATOR POWER

SIZE: Bell up to 11.8 in (30 cm) wide; tentacles up to 9.8 ft (3 m) long when fully extended

DISTRIBUTION: Tropical and subtropical open-ocean waters worldwide

DIET: Fish and other small planktonic animals

LION'S MANE JELLYFISH

Cyanea capillata

Massive bell pulsates to propel the animal through water

This giant among jellyfish can weigh up to a ton. It is a cold-water animal, preferring to stay close to Arctic ice, although individuals may drift long distances, and sometimes wash ashore in other parts of the world. Swarms of this jellyfish occasionally gather in the open ocean.

This is the world's **biggest species** of jellyfish.

Tight cluster of more than one thousand tentacles resembles a lion's mane

DATA FILE

 PREDATOR POWER

 SIZE: Bell up to 7.5 ft (2.3 m) wide; tentacles up to 121.4 ft (37 m) long when fully extended

 DISTRIBUTION: Cold open-ocean waters of North Atlantic and North Pacific oceans

 DIET: Fish and other jellyfish

Cruisers and chasers

PORTUGUESE MAN O' WAR
Physalia physalis

Gas-filled float catches ocean breezes, like a sail

Although it looks like a jellyfish, the Portuguese Man o' War is a colony of tentacle-like animals hanging from a balloon-like float. The longest tentacles are muscular stingers that grab prey. Other structures have mouths for swallowing paralyzed fish, or organs for producing eggs.

DATA FILE

PREDATOR POWER
! ! ! !

SIZE: Float up to 11.8 in (30 cm) long; tentacles up to 164 ft (50 m) long when fully extended

DISTRIBUTION: Tropical and subtropical open-ocean waters worldwide

DIET: Fish and other invertebrates

Parts of the colony—called zooids—hang in tentacles from the float

The colony can **deflate its float** to submerge briefly.

BARREL SHRIMP

Phronima sp.

The barrel shrimp has a grotesque life history. It gets its name because the female preys on floating "jellies," scooping out their insides and using the barrel-shaped husk as a brooding chamber for her eggs. She pushes the barrel around with her, like a stroller, until the eggs hatch.

Husk of dead salp used as brooding chamber

Large head has strong biting mouthparts

This predator has inspired **monster movies**.

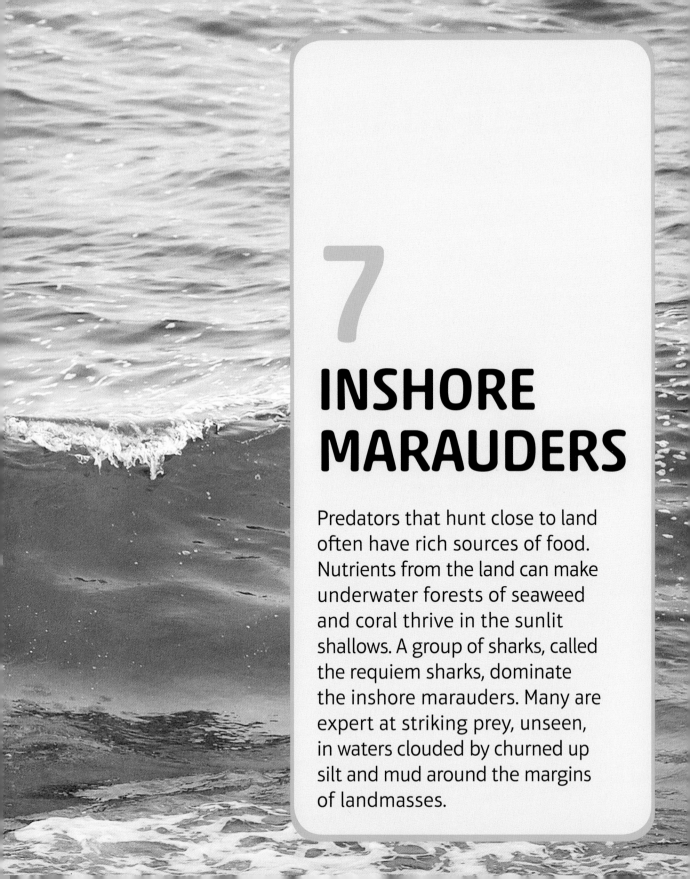

7

INSHORE MARAUDERS

Predators that hunt close to land often have rich sources of food. Nutrients from the land can make underwater forests of seaweed and coral thrive in the sunlit shallows. A group of sharks, called the requiem sharks, dominate the inshore marauders. Many are expert at striking prey, unseen, in waters clouded by churned up silt and mud around the margins of landmasses.

AUSTRALIAN
SWELL SHARK
Cephaloscyllium laticeps

One of several kinds of swell shark that are found in warm regions throughout the world, the Australian swell shark inflates its stomach by gulping in water when danger threatens. This helps to wedge it inside rocky crevices, so a predator cannot pull it free.

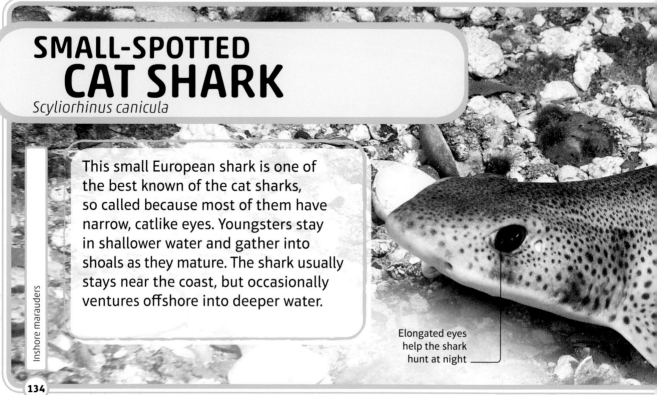

SMALL-SPOTTED
CAT SHARK
Scyliorhinus canicula

This small European shark is one of the best known of the cat sharks, so called because most of them have narrow, catlike eyes. Youngsters stay in shallower water and gather into shoals as they mature. The shark usually stays near the coast, but occasionally ventures offshore into deeper water.

Elongated eyes help the shark hunt at night

Inshore marauders

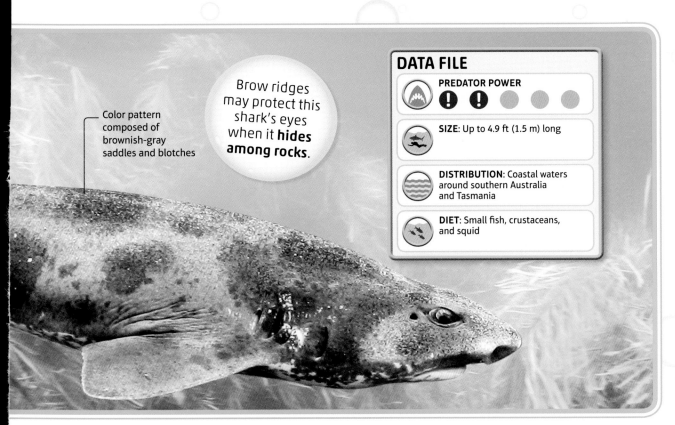

Color pattern composed of brownish-gray saddles and blotches

Brow ridges may protect this shark's eyes when it **hides among rocks**.

DATA FILE

PREDATOR POWER

SIZE: Up to 4.9 ft (1.5 m) long

DISTRIBUTION: Coastal waters around southern Australia and Tasmania

DIET: Small fish, crustaceans, and squid

Adults often live in **single-sex schools**.

Body covered in small, dark spots

DATA FILE

PREDATOR POWER

SIZE: Up to 3.3 ft (1 m) long

DISTRIBUTION: Coastal waters of north-eastern Atlantic Ocean and Mediterranean Sea

DIET: Bottom-living crustaceans, snails, squid, worms, and fish

Inshore marauders

CORAL
CAT SHARK
Atelomycterus marmoratus

This shark is a **popular choice** for **aquariums**.

The coral cat shark's body is so narrow that it can set up home between the rocks of a coral reef, among which it lives by day. Its spotted pattern also provides good camouflage against the reef background. Only at night does this shark emerge to hunt small animals, often returning to the same hiding place by daybreak.

Narrow body makes it easy for shark to enter between small gaps in coral to hunt for food

Long, eellike body with black blotches and scattered, white spots

DATA FILE

PREDATOR POWER

SIZE: Up to 27.5 in (70 cm) long

DISTRIBUTION: Coral reefs along Pakistan and India, and Southeast Asia to New Guinea

FEEDING: Mollusks, crustaceans, and small fish

Inshore marauders

PYJAMA SHARK
Poroderma africanum

No other shark has the stripy, pyjama-like costume of this little hunter. Like most other cat sharks, the pyjama shark is a nocturnal hunter, active at night. It prefers rocky areas in which there are plenty of caves for shelter, but it may sometimes venture into very shallow water in the seashore's intertidal zone (the area under water at high tide).

DATA FILE

PREDATOR POWER

SIZE: Up to 3.3 ft (1 m) long

DISTRIBUTION: Shallow coastal waters of South Africa

FEEDING: Fish and invertebrates

Dark stripes run down the length of the body

Narrow eyes are higher on the head than in many other cat sharks

This shark can **tear tentacles** from a small octopus.

Inshore marauders

RED-SPOTTED CAT SHARK
Schroederichthys chilensis

Like many other kinds of cat shark, the red-spotted cat shark from South America has a blotchy skin pattern. At times the blotches intensify and can break up the outline of the fish, especially against the background of the kelp (seaweed) fronds found in its shoreline habitat. Despite its name, the spots on its skin are brown, rather than red.

Dark "saddles" at intervals along the body

Dark brown spots outnumber white spots

This shark can **stay absolutely still** when picked up by divers.

DATA FILE

PREDATOR POWER
❗ ❗

SIZE: Up to 27.6 in (70 cm) long

DISTRIBUTION: Shallow coastal waters along the Pacific coast of Peru and Chile

DIET: Small crustaceans and other invertebrates

Inshore marauders

PUFFADDER SHY SHARK

Haploblepharus edwardsii

Shy sharks form a group of small, mainly brightly patterned, sharks from South Africa that get their name from an extraordinary response to danger. When threatened, they curl up into a ring and cover their eyes with their tail. The puffadder shy shark lives on sandy or rocky bottoms, usually close to the shore, and often in groups.

The **curled-up posture** may stop bigger sharks from taking a bite.

Golden-brown "saddles" with darker margins

Small, white blotches scattered across body

DATA FILE

 PREDATOR POWER

 SIZE: Up to 23.6 in (60 cm) long

 HABITAT: Shallow coastal waters of South Africa

 DIET: Fish, crustaceans, squid, and worms

GREY-SPOTTED
CAT SHARK
Asymbolus analis

This small shark is found only in the coastal waters of eastern Australia. Like many other cat sharks, the grey-spotted cat shark frequently approaches the shoreline in shallow water. However, it is less common than other small sharks that live in the same habitat, so little is known about its habits.

The grey-spotted cat shark lays **vase-shaped egg cases**.

DATA FILE

PREDATOR POWER
❗ ❗

SIZE: Up to 24 in (61 cm) long

DISTRIBUTION: Coastal waters of eastern Australia

DIET: Fish, crustaceans, and squid

Light and dark brown spots and saddles

Slightly flattened, rounded head

Inshore marauders

BLACK-MOUTHED CAT SHARK

Galeus melastomus

The black-mouthed cat shark lives in deeper water than many cat sharks, swimming in the ocean where the continental shelf drops sharply toward the abyss. Here, its sensitive vision can follow the glow of animals, such as the lanternfish. This shark sticks close to the bottom and uses its long body to swim with slow, eellike undulations.

Large eyes

Dark saddles, blotches, and circular spots run the length of the body

Female black-mouthed cat sharks lay up to **100 egg cases** each year.

DATA FILE

 PREDATOR POWER

 SIZE: Up to 35.4 in (90 cm) long

 DISTRIBUTION: Coastal waters of northeastern Atlantic Ocean, North Sea, and Mediterranean Sea

 DIET: Lanternfish and bottom-living invertebrates, such as shrimps and squid

Inshore marauders

BIG-EYED
HOUND SHARK
Iago omanensis

The extra-long gill slits of the big-eyed hound shark may help it survive in warm waters, in which oxygen levels are too low to support other kinds of shark. This fish can also tolerate higher salt concentrations than other sharks. It lives in the Red Sea, and a related species lives in the Bay of Bengal.

Gills inside these long slits can extract plenty of oxygen

Large, green eyes help this shark hunt in dark water

TOPE
SHARK
Galeorhinus galeus

A tope shark has migrated a record distance of **1,569 miles (2,525 km)**.

Topes are closely related to inshore reef sharks, but wander much further out to sea. The common tope's urge to migrate sees it travel long distances regularly. These sharks prefer lower sea temperatures. They either move away from the equator during the warmest months, or go into deeper, cooler waters.

Inshore marauders

The males live in **deeper waters** than the females.

DATA FILE

PREDATOR POWER
! !

SIZE: Up to 22.8 in (58 cm) long

DISTRIBUTION: Warm coastal waters of Red Sea, Gulf of Oman, and possibly Bay of Bengal

DIET: Fish, squid, and octopuses

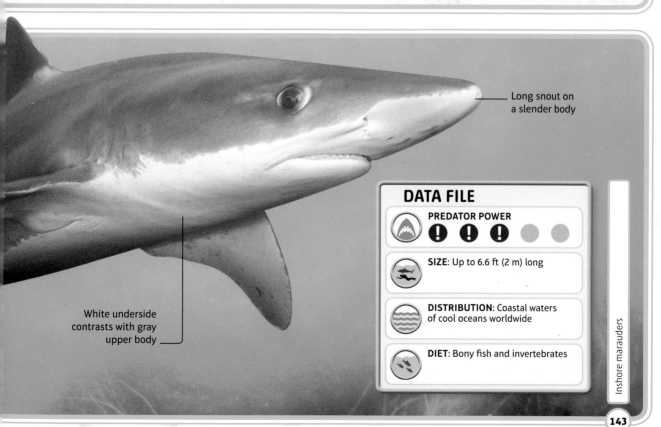

Long snout on a slender body

White underside contrasts with gray upper body

DATA FILE

PREDATOR POWER
! ! !

SIZE: Up to 6.6 ft (2 m) long

DISTRIBUTION: Coastal waters of cool oceans worldwide

DIET: Bony fish and invertebrates

LEOPARD SHARK
Triakis semifasciata

Leopard sharks can **tear a clam** from **its shell**.

Center of each dark, saddle-like marking gets paler as the shark matures

Broad, rounded snout

This strikingly patterned North American shark lives in shallow waters with low oxygen levels, such as around bays and estuaries. The leopard shark likes to follow the ebb and flow of the tide in search of mud-living prey and is often seen in the company of other similar-sized sharks. Females venture into eelgrass beds in water less than three feet deep to give birth.

DATA FILE

 **PREDATOR POWER** ❗ ❗ ● ● ●

SIZE: Up to 5.9 ft (1.8 m) long

DISTRIBUTION: Shallow coastal waters and estuaries along the Pacific coast of North America

DIET: Crabs, clams, worms, and fish

Inshore marauders

STARRY
SMOOTH HOUND

Mustelus asterias

The starry smooth hound gets its name from the small, white, starlike spots on its body, although, in many cases, these markings may be faint. It swims over sand and gravel, and migrates further inshore during summer months. Like its close relatives, this shark uses its crushing jaws and teeth to feed on crabs and other crustaceans.

DATA FILE

 PREDATOR POWER
❗ ❗ ● ● ●

 SIZE: Up to 4.6 ft (1.4 m) long

 DISTRIBUTION: Coastal waters of north-eastern Atlantic Ocean and Mediterranean Sea

 DIET: Crustaceans

Gray or brownish body
lacks darker markings

Tiny,
starlike
spots

This shark uses its small, **grinding teeth** to **crunch** the **shells of crabs**.

GUMMY
SHARK
Mustelus antarcticus

Sometimes a predator needs jaws for crunching, rather than for slicing. This species of hound shark has flat teeth for cracking the hard shells of crustaceans. It swims near the bottom around the cooler parts of Australia, where females give birth in shallow nurseries.

Jaws are packed with flat teeth for crushing hard-shelled prey

BANDED
HOUND SHARK
Triakis scyllium

Like most members of the hound shark family, this species has a restricted range of distribution—in coastal waters around Japan and eastern Asia. This suggests this shark rarely travels long distances. It is especially common in muddy estuaries and bays, where it lives among seaweeds and eelgrass.

Inshore marauders

Small, dark spots and blotches

Small, white spots on a bronze- or gray-colored body

DATA FILE

PREDATOR POWER

SIZE: Up to 5.9 ft (1.8 m) long

DISTRIBUTION: Waters off southern Australia and Tasmania

DIET: Crustaceans, worms, and fish

The gummy shark has a maximum **lifespan of 16 years**.

Short, rounded snout

DATA FILE

PREDATOR POWER

SIZE: Up to 4.9 ft (1.5 m) long

DISTRIBUTION: Coastal waters of Japan and eastern Asia

DIET: Small fish, crustaceans, and other invertebrates

The banded hound shark gives birth to **up to 24 pups per litter**.

Inshore marauders

TIGER SHARK

Galeocerdo cuvier

The tiger shark has been nicknamed the "garbage can of the ocean" for good reason. As it patrols coastlines, it will guzzle on anything in the water that it thinks might be edible. As well as its usual fishy prey, it may also attack animals from the land. Amazingly, this shark will even swallow human trash!

Large mouth contains saw-edged teeth

Vertical bars resembling tiger stripes may fade in older, bigger sharks

Pure white belly contrasts with gray side and upper body

Keel on side of body, near tail, improves swimming speed

This shark is responsible for some **fatal attacks** on **humans**.

DATA FILE

PREDATOR POWER
❗ ❗ ❗ ❗ ❗

SIZE: Up to 24.3 ft (7.4 m) long

DISTRIBUTION: Coastal waters of tropical and warm, temperate oceans, and Mediterranean Sea

DIET: Fish, turtles, seabirds, seals, dolphins, sea snakes, and invertebrates

Inshore marauders

LEMON SHARK

Negaprion brevirostris

Warm, sunny lagoons are the favorite habitat of this tropical hunter. After mating, pregnant female lemon sharks gather in the lagoons of the Caribbean to give birth. Baby lemon sharks will spend their early years here, growing up in the safety of a tropical nursery.

DATA FILE

 PREDATOR POWER
 ❗ ❗ ❗ ● ●

 SIZE: Up to 11.2 ft (3.4 m) long

 HABITAT: Warm, shallow coastal waters of tropical Atlantic and Pacific oceans

 DIET: Fish and, sometimes, seabirds

Up to **500 baby lemon sharks** can live in a single nursery.

Lemon-yellow tinge of color is best seen in sunlit lagoons

Bluntly rounded snout

Lemon shark, side view

BULL SHARK
Carcharhinus leucas

Big, triangular, first dorsal fin may stick out of the water when the shark is in the shallows _____

The bull shark lives in coastal waters that are often made murky by mud running in from the land, but it regularly goes beyond the estuaries to swim up rivers. Adventurous bull sharks can travel thousands of miles inland, sometimes crossing rapids to do so.

DATA FILE

PREDATOR POWER

SIZE: Up to 11 ft (3.4 m) long

DISTRIBUTION: Coastal waters and rivers, and in tropical and warm, temperate oceans

DIET: Fish, crustaceans, turtles, echinoderms, birds, and mammals

Inshore marauders

150

Large, thick head has small eyes and a short snout

Bull shark, side view

Bull sharks may be **attracted to human activity** on the shore.

SARCASTIC FRINGEHEAD

Neoclinus blanchardi

Fighting fringeheads push their jaws together, **as though kissing**.

The extraordinary threat display of this fish is worse than its bite. The fringehead spends much of its time in a burrow, occasionally coming out to hunt shrimps and small crabs. If two fringeheads come face to face, they flare out their jaws to show that each is the boss of its own territory.

DATA FILE

 PREDATOR POWER

 SIZE: Up to 11.8 in (30 cm) long

 DISTRIBUTION: Coastal waters off California

 DIET: Crustaceans

Much of the eellike body is concealed inside a burrow or tube

Fringehead, top view

ATLANTIC
WOLF-FISH

Anarhichas lupus

The formidable jaws and teeth of the wolf-fish are good for eating snails, crabs, and sea urchins. Crunching through hard shells is no problem for this cold-water predator. Unlike most oceanic bony fish—which scatter their eggs in the water for fertilization—this fish has internal fertilization. The males protect the brood in a nest for several months.

DATA FILE

 PREDATOR POWER
  ● ● ●

 SIZE: Up to 4.9 ft (1.5 m) long

 DISTRIBUTION: Cold coastal waters of North Atlantic Ocean

 DIET: Mollusks, crustaceans, and echinoderms

A substance in this fish's blood keeps it **flowing in the cold**.

Daggerlike teeth at the front are so big they protrude from the mouth

Atlantic wolf-fish, side view

Inshore marauders

153

KILLER WHALE
Orcinus orca

The killer whale, also called orca, is the biggest member of the dolphin family. Like other dolphins, it has a taste for fish. However, it hunts big marine mammals too, and regularly comes close to the shoreline on the trail of seals. Killer whales travel together in groups called "pods," which sometimes consist of more than 50 individuals.

Dorsal fin in adult is the biggest of any marine mammal, and is as tall as an adult human. The dorsal fin of males is much bigger than that of females (female in image).

Killer whale, side view

Black upper side contrasts sharply with white underside and patches behind eyes

DATA FILE

PREDATOR POWER
❗ ❗ ❗ ❗ ❗

SIZE: Up to 31.2 ft (9.5 m) long

DISTRIBUTION: Coastal waters worldwide, but mainly in cooler regions

DIET: Fish, squid, seals, dolphins, and marine birds

Killer whales **hunt in teams** to catch seals.

LEOPARD SEAL
Hydrurga leptonyx

Most kinds of seals hunt fish only, but the leopard seal sometimes likes meatier prey. Although its teeth are not as daggerlike as those of many land carnivores, its jaws are very strong, and it is capable of killing a penguin by shaking it. This seal waits to grab a penguin as it jumps into the water, and sometimes smacks it on the water's surface to knock it senseless.

Stocky head with strong jaws

Scattered, dark spots give the leopard seal its name

The leopard seal **interlocks its teeth** to strain krill from the water.

Leopard seal, side view

DATA FILE

 PREDATOR POWER
! ! ! ! !

 SIZE: Up to 11.2 ft (3.4 m) long

 DISTRIBUTION: Rocky coastlines and coastal waters around Antarctica

 DIET: Fish, squid and octopuses, krill, other seals, and penguins

SOUTHERN ELEPHANT SEAL

Mirounga leonina

This seal is the **heaviest land-going marine carnivore**.

An elephant seal can spend up to eight months of the year out at sea fishing for food. This giant among seals can dive more than 0.6 miles (1 km) below the surface for fish, and can hold its breath for up to two hours—longer than most other marine mammals. However, when it is time to breed, the southern elephant seal returns to shore to mate and give birth, like other seals.

DATA FILE

 PREDATOR POWER

 SIZE: 9.8–16.4 ft (3–5 m) long; males are bigger, and much heavier, than females

 DISTRIBUTION: Coastlines and coastal ocean waters of Antarctica and southern tip of South America

 DIET: Fish and squid

Males use their fleshy proboscis (long nose) to louden their roar

Southern elephant seal, side view

SEA
OTTER
Enhydris lutris

PREDATOR POWER

SIZE: Up to 4.9 ft (1.5 m) long

HABITAT: North Pacific shorelines and coastal waters of Russia and North America

DIET: Mollusks, crabs, and sea urchins

The sea otter is the smallest marine mammal. It lacks the thick blubber of bigger ocean mammals, so stays warm in cold Pacific waters with a fur coat so dense that little of the animal's precious body heat escapes. Sea otters pick up rocks with their front paws and use them to smash open clams and other prey. They can even do this on the flat of their bellies while floating on their back in the water.

Sea otter, front view

Dense fur keeps otter warm, so it can float on its back in icy water

Sea otters have the **densest fur of any mammal**.

Inshore marauders

EMPEROR PENGUIN
Aptenodytes forsteri

Small feathers trap air close to the body to help with insulation

This is the only animal that **breeds on mainland Antarctica** during winter.

Wings flap up and down for propulsion

Emperor penguin, side view

Emperor penguins hunt fish in the icy waters around Antarctica, but, remarkably, also journey into the frozen continent on foot to breed. Here the males endure the bitter polar winter as they incubate their eggs, waiting for the females to bring a meal of fish once the eggs have hatched.

DATA FILE

PREDATOR POWER

SIZE: Up to 3.9 ft (1.2 m) high

HABITAT: Shorelines and coastal waters of Antarctica

DIET: Fish, squid, and krill

Inshore marauders

SALTWATER **CROCODILE**
Crocodylus porosus

The world's largest reptile, the saltwater crocodile is a predator of tropical swamplands. It can snatch large mammals from the waterside, pulling them into the water, while rolling over to drown its prey. Unlike other crocodilians, it tolerates saltwater, so regularly swims out to sea, sometimes reaching remote oceanic islands.

Saltwater crocodiles can stay submerged in water for **up to 2 hours**.

Darker markings on yellowish scales fade as animal grows older

DATA FILE

PREDATOR POWER
❗ ❗ ❗ ❗ ❗

SIZE: Up to 20.3 ft (6.2 m) long

DISTRIBUTION: Rivers, estuaries, and coastlines of India, Southeast Asia, New Guinea, and Australia

DIET: Mammals, birds, and fish

Eyes have a transparent third eyelid, called a nictitating membrane

Unlike in alligators, the fourth tooth of the lower jaw pokes into a notch in the upper jaw

Inshore marauders

SEA SNAKE

Hydrophis sp.

Probably no other reptile is as well adapted to ocean life as a sea snake. Unlike turtles, which have to lay eggs on land, sea snakes give birth to live young in the water. These snakes are close relatives of land cobras and share their potent venom, using it to immobilize their prey.

Sea snakes have **one of the strongest venoms** of any snake.

Paddle-like tail propels snake in water

No enlarged belly scales for gripping ground, such as in land-living snakes

Inshore marauders

NAUTILUS

Nautilus pompilius

The nautilus is often described as a "living fossil," because it has changed very little over millions of years of evolution. It belongs to a group of animals called cephalopods, which includes the squid and octopus. Its tentacles are too feeble to tackle big prey, and its jet-propelled swimming movements are rather sluggish.

DATA FILE

 PREDATOR POWER
 ❗ ❗ ● ● ●

 SIZE: Up to 7.9 in (20 cm) long

 DISTRIBUTION: Tropical coastal waters of Indian and western Pacific oceans

DIET: Crustaceans, other small, slow-moving animals, and dead animals

Jet propulsion helps it move backward in water.

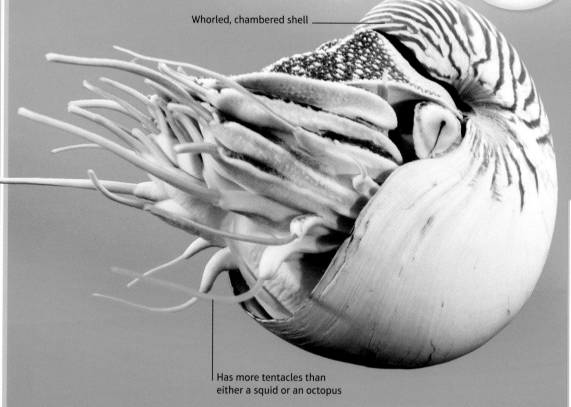

Whorled, chambered shell

Has more tentacles than either a squid or an octopus

Inshore marauders

PEACOCK MANTIS SHRIMP

Odontodactylus scyllarus

Highly sophisticated eyes provide the most complex color vision of any animal

A mantis shrimp can **smash its way out** of an aquarium.

Claws modified into clubs

There are two kinds of mantis shrimp—stabbers and smashers. Stabbers have spiny claws that spear prey, but the colorful peacock mantis shrimp uses a club to smash through shells. The mantis shrimp lives in a burrow, the entrance of which is usually littered with the broken fragments of its prey.

DATA FILE

PREDATOR POWER

SIZE: Up to 7.1 in (18 cm) long

DISTRIBUTION: Tropical coastal waters of Indian and western Pacific oceans

DIET: Shelled mollusks and crustaceans

Inshore marauders

SMOOTH-CLAWED
PISTOL SHRIMP
Alpheus paracrinitus

The snapping pincers make **much of the underwater noise** in the ocean.

This little shrimp disables prey in a remarkable way. It has a special claw that can snap shut with such speed and force that it generates shock waves. These are powerful enough to stun small animals nearby. The shrimp then drags the immobile victims into its lair to eat them alive.

Bold, colored patterns

Enlarged pincer generates shock waves

DATA FILE

 PREDATOR POWER
❗ ❗ ● ● ●

 SIZE: Up to 0.7 in (1.8 cm) long

 DISTRIBUTION: Tropical reefs of Atlantic Ocean and Caribbean Sea

 DIET: Other small crustaceans and small fish

Inshore marauders

8

PREDATORS OF THE REEF

Tropical coral reefs are extremely rich in ocean life. Coral not only forms an ocean habitat, but is itself a predator. In warm, sunny waters, it grows into huge rocky colonies, which are covered in billions of plankton-grabbing tentacles. Many predators live on the reef, including many species of shark.

BLACKTIP SHARK
Carcharhinus limbatus

Fin tips are often black, but the markings may fade in older sharks

The blacktip shark thrives in shallow waters around estuaries and muddy mangrove swamps. It is an acrobatic predator that gathers in large numbers to charge at shoaling fish. When doing this, blacktip sharks will sometimes jump right out of the water and spin around in midair.

The blacktip shark can **spin three times** when it jumps out of the water.

DATA FILE

 PREDATOR POWER

 SIZE: Up to 8.5 ft (2.6 m) long

DISTRIBUTION: Coral reefs of warm, temperate and tropical oceans, and Mediterranean and Red seas

 DIET: Fish, crustaceans, and squid

OCEANIC
WHITETIP SHARK
Carcharhinus longimanus

One of the most abundant of all sharks, the oceanic whitetip shark is especially common around remote islands, but can also wander far from the shore. It is not as speedy as some other open-ocean sharks, but it is more aggressive around prey, especially when it gathers together in groups.

Long, paddle-like pectoral fins spread wide as the shark cruises beneath the ocean surface

The whitetip shark **bullies smaller sharks** at feeding frenzies.

DATA FILE

PREDATOR POWER

SIZE: Up to 12.8 ft (3.9 m) long

DISTRIBUTION: Surface waters of open oceans and island coastlines in tropical and subtropical regions

DIET: Large fish, squid, seabirds, and mammals

SILKY SHARK
Carcharhinus falciformis

Most of the silky sharks seen swimming over reefs close to the shore are likely to be immature ones. As individuals of this species grow older, they spend more time in the open ocean. The silky shark has especially sensitive hearing, which helps it home in on the deep, rumbling sounds coming from a shark feeding frenzy.

The silky shark's **smooth skin** gives this hunter its name.

Smooth skin is due to network of tiny, densely-packed denticles (tiny, toothlike scales)

Upper body may appear blackish

Long, narrow pectoral fin

DUSKY **SHARK**
Carcharhinus obscurus

The dusky shark can often be seen **tailing ships**.

Gray- or bronze-colored upper body

Dusky-tipped fin is not as boldly marked as in some other related species

Like many of the related reef sharks, the dusky shark likes warm waters, although it migrates away from the tropics during the hottest months of the year. Females move closer to shore to give birth to their pups. Here, the youngsters will gather in shoals before they grow into adults and venture out into deeper water.

DATA FILE

 PREDATOR POWER

 SIZE: Up to 13.1 ft (4 m) long

 DISTRIBUTION: Coastal waters in tropical and warm, temperate oceans worldwide

 DIET: Fish (including other sharks) and crustaceans

Predators of the reef

GALAPAGOS SHARK

Carcharhinus galapagensis

This shark may **hunch its back** to threaten nearby divers.

Gray-brown upper body fades to whitish below

Large, sickle-shaped pectoral fins may have dusky tips

Despite its name, the Galapagos shark is not confined to the Pacific Ocean's Galapagos Islands, but lives around most tropical islands on Earth. It apparently favors rocky habitats, in which the currents can be especially strong. This shark swims in groups and has a reputation for being aggressive, even dominating other kinds of shark near prey.

DATA FILE

 PREDATOR POWER

SIZE: Possibly up to 12.1 ft (3.7 m) long

DISTRIBUTION: Coastal waters around islands in warm, temperate and tropical oceans worldwide

DIET: Mainly bottom-living fish

CARIBBEAN REEF SHARK

Carcharhinus perezi

The Caribbean reef shark lies motionless, seemingly asleep, in caves or on the ocean floor. This allows divers to approach it, making it quite popular with tourist divers. This tropical American predator uses the muscles at the back of its throat to pump water over its gills, supplying them with oxygen.

Upper body is dark grayish or brownish in color

Faint, white band on the side of the body near the rear, like in related sharks

Large, narrow pectoral fins

DATA FILE

 PREDATOR POWER

 SIZE: Up to 9.8 ft (3 m) long

 DISTRIBUTION: Coastal waters and river mouths of western Atlantic Ocean and Caribbean Sea

 DIET: Fish

This docile shark only **rarely tries to bite** human divers.

BLACKTIP
REEF SHARK
Carcharhinus melanopterus

One of the most common species of reef shark in the tropical Indo-Pacific, the blacktip reef shark is a fast-moving predator. It stays in midwater or close to the bottom, but sometimes moves into the shallows, where its dorsal fin can be seen sticking up out of the water. It even occasionally ventures into brackish (slightly salty) waters of estuaries.

Prominent black fin tips are underlined with white

White band runs along side of body toward the rear

Short, rounded snout

DATA FILE

 PREDATOR POWER
! ! !

 SIZE: Up to 6.6 ft (2 m) long

 DISTRIBUTION: Coral reefs of tropical Indian and western Pacific oceans, and Mediterranean and Red seas

 DIET: Fish, crustaceans, squid, and mollusks

This shark will not leave its **favorite patch** of reef for **years on end**.

GRAY
REEF SHARK
Carcharhinus amblyrhynchos

Very popular with tourists, the gray reef shark is a highly common reef shark in the tropics. It swims in groups in shallow water and is sometimes curious enough to approach divers. At night, the groups seem to get more restless and disperse into more open waters.

White underside contrasts with gray upper body

Pregnant female **gray reef sharks** may gather in **large groups**.

Black-tipped fins

DATA FILE

 PREDATOR POWER

 SIZE: Possibly up to 8.2 ft (2.5 m) long

 DISTRIBUTION: Coastal waters of the tropical and warm, temperate Indian and western Pacific oceans

 DIET: Fish, squid, octopuses, and crustaceans

BRONZE WHALER
Carcharhinus brachyurus

Grayish upper body has a bronze sheen

The bronze whaler **grows slower** than most other kinds of shark.

Long pectoral fins

Black fin edges may be clearer on some fins than others

Each year large numbers of the bronze whaler gather along the East African coast to follow the sardine run, a seasonal northward migration of massive shoals of sardines that attracts many of the ocean's predators. Bronze whalers in other parts of the world also make small migrations, but the reasons are not always clear.

DATA FILE

 PREDATOR POWER

 SIZE: Up to 9.5 ft (2.9 m) long

 DISTRIBUTION: Coastal waters of Atlantic, Pacific, and Indian oceans, and Mediterranean Sea

 DIET: Fish, squid, and octopuses

BLUE SHARK

Prionace glauca

Unlike the related reef sharks, the blue shark spends much of its life away from coastlines. By hunting in groups, it can make shoals of prey bunch together, even in the wide expanse of the open ocean. These hunters take turns to grab a mouthful from the gathered prey.

Often hunting in packs, blue sharks are called the **"wolves of the sea."**

Long, narrow pectoral fins are good for turning at speed while swimming

These sharks feed predominantly at night and probably use their large, well-developed eyes at close range to detect bioluminescence

DATA FILE

 PREDATOR POWER

 SIZE: Up to 12.5 ft (3.8 m) long

 DISTRIBUTION: Open ocean worldwide, except in the coldest regions, and Mediterranean Sea

 DIET: Fish, squid, other invertebrates, and seabirds

Predators of the reef

WHITETIP REEF SHARK

Triaenodon obesus

The whitetip reef shark prowls the rocky crevices of a tropical reef in search of prey. Small fish dart between rocks that provide a safe hiding spot, but this shark's small, slender body is perfect for reaching them. Sometimes, if the shark fails to make a grab straight away, it waits patiently between the rocks until its prey emerges.

Slender body and extra tough skin help the shark hunt easily among rocks

Strong brow ridges protect the eyes of the shark as it probes between rocks for prey

DATA FILE

 PREDATOR POWER

 SIZE: Up to 5.2 ft (1.6 m) long

 DISTRIBUTION: Coral reefs of tropical Indian and Pacific oceans, and Red Sea

 DIET: Fish, octopuses, lobsters, and crabs

White tip on dorsal fin

This shark **rarely travels** more than **1.86 miles (3 km)** from home in a year.

GREAT
HAMMERHEAD
Sphyrna mokarran

The great hammerhead shark may swim over coral reefs, but it often goes further into the open ocean on its journey to new coastlines. Like other hammerheads, the great hammerhead sweeps the ocean bottom with its "hammer" to sense bottom-living prey and has a particular taste for stingrays.

Enormous, first dorsal fin stands higher than those of any other hammerhead

Distinct notch in the center of the "hammer"

The great hammerhead is the **biggest of all** the hammerhead sharks.

Pectoral and pelvic fins curve back strongly along their rear margins

DATA FILE

PREDATOR POWER

SIZE: Up to 20 ft (6.1 m) long

DISTRIBUTION: Coastal waters of tropical and warm, temperate oceans worldwide

DIET: Stingrays, groupers, and sea catfish

Predators of the reef

SCALLOPED HAMMERHEAD

Sphyrna lewini

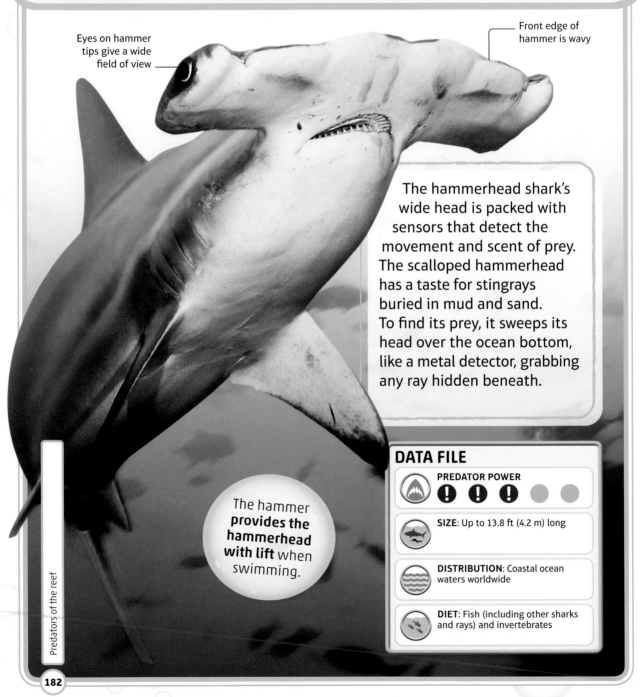

Eyes on hammer tips give a wide field of view

Front edge of hammer is wavy

The hammerhead shark's wide head is packed with sensors that detect the movement and scent of prey. The scalloped hammerhead has a taste for stingrays buried in mud and sand. To find its prey, it sweeps its head over the ocean bottom, like a metal detector, grabbing any ray hidden beneath.

The hammer **provides the hammerhead with lift** when swimming.

DATA FILE

PREDATOR POWER
❗ ❗ ❗ ● ●

SIZE: Up to 13.8 ft (4.2 m) long

DISTRIBUTION: Coastal ocean waters worldwide

DIET: Fish (including other sharks and rays) and invertebrates

CROWN-OF-THORNS STARFISH
Acanthaster planci

Here is the ultimate enemy of coral. It is one of the biggest of all starfish and has an appetite to match. It creeps on tiny tube feet over the surface of a coral colony, nibbling away at the fleshy polyps. Few animals can eat this starfish, and so heavy infestations of the crown-of-thorns can cause serious damage to a reef.

DATA FILE

    PREDATOR POWER

 SIZE: Up to 27.6 in (70 cm) in diameter

 DISTRIBUTION: Tropical coastal waters of Indian and Pacific oceans, and Red Sea

 DIET: Coral reef polyps

Spines can transfer poison, causing swelling and pain to human skin

Up to 21 arms

A single starfish **can kill 64.6 sq ft (6 sq m)** of coral in a year.

GREEN MORAY EEL
Gymnothorax funebris

Morays include the biggest kinds of eel. Most live in rocky lairs on coral reefs and rely on surprise to ambush passing prey. Some morays seem to cooperate with predatory grouper fish in driving prey into the open from between rocks—so both hunters end up with a share of the meal.

Mouth is kept open to keep water moving through small gill openings

Morays have an **extra set of jaws** in their throat that pop out to grab prey.

Yellowish or greenish color comes from a protective mucus coating

x

DATA FILE

 PREDATOR POWER

 SIZE: Up to 8.2 ft (2.5 m) long

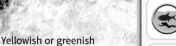 **DISTRIBUTION:** Tropical coastal waters of the Gulf of Mexico and Caribbean Sea

 DIET: Fish, crabs, squid, and shrimps

HUMPHEAD WRASSE
Cheilinus undulatus

This reef-dwelling fish is a big, unfussy predator and will tackle prey that many other hunters find distasteful or even poisonous. Juveniles usually stay hidden among rocks and seaweed, but big adults patrol more open water on the edge of the reef. Adults change sex when they reach maturity, turning from female to male after about nine years.

This fish may **eat poisonous animals**, such as crown-of-thorns starfish.

Forehead hump is prominent in bigger, older individuals _____

Thick, fleshy lips

Predators of the reef

BRAIN CORAL
Colpophyllia natans

Coral may look like lifeless rock, but in fact it is a colony of tiny predators. At night, its rocky skeleton comes alive with thousands of tiny polyps. Each polyp is like a miniature anemone, with a ring of little tentacles for catching plankton, and a central mouth for swallowing the tiny meal.

Coral colonies **release eggs and sperms simultaneously**.

Ridges of the skeleton make the colony's surface look like a human brain

Predators of the reef

MAGNIFICENT
SEA ANEMONE
Heteractis magnifica

Clown fish families often live in the **tentacles of sea anemones**.

Anemones may look like plants, but they are actually predatory animals. Their muscular tentacles are armed with microscopic stingers that paralyse small prey. The magnificent sea anemone supplements this diet by making use of algae that live in its flesh. These use light energy in bright sunlight to provide sugar through a process called photosynthesis.

Stinging tentacles catch plankton and transfer it to the mouth in the center

DATA FILE

 PREDATOR POWER

 SIZE: Up to 19.7 in (50 cm) in diameter

 DISTRIBUTION: Coral reefs of tropical Indian and western Pacific oceans, and Red Sea

 DIET: Small invertebrates and tiny fish; some food is made by algae living in the anemone's flesh

Column contains the stomach for digesting prey

HARLEQUIN SHRIMP

Hymenocera picta

This colorful, little shrimp has a taste for starfish flesh and little else, and will go to extraordinary lengths to get a meal. The harlequin shrimp is strong and nimble enough to carry a small starfish back to its burrow. Once there, it uses the starfish as a kind of living pantry, feeding on it one leg at a time.

 PREDATOR POWER

 SIZE: Up to 2 in (5 cm) long

 DISTRIBUTION: Tropical coastal waters of Indian and western Pacific oceans

DIET: Starfish and sometimes sea urchins

Sharp claws help tear starfish into pieces

Sensory antennae can "taste" the water for prey

This shrimp can flip a starfish **onto its back** to nibble on its soft underside.

ANNA'S SEA SLUG
Chromodoris annae

Hornlike gills at the rear of the body

Bright colors warn predators that this sea slug might be poisonous

Sensory club on the head projects into the water

Anna's sea slugs can **"smell"** sponge prey with their **sensory clubs**.

Not all predators on a reef gobble down their prey in one go. Like land snails, sea slugs feed by rasping away at stationary food. Anna's sea slug prefers to eat sponges, a type of colonial animal that grows fixed on rocks. Other sea slugs munch on stinging anemones and even use the stingers for their own protection.

DATA FILE

PREDATOR POWER
!

SIZE: Up to 2 in (5 cm) long

DISTRIBUTION: Tropical coastal waters of western Pacific Ocean

DIET: Sponges

REFERENCE

Sharks include some of the most formidable predators of the ocean. Practically every ocean habitat, from the intertidal shallows to the deepest abyss, is home to sharks. Their family tree extends back hundreds of millions of years, but these are no primitive survivors of a bygone age—modern sharks have sharp senses for finding prey and sophisticated ways of raising their young.

THE SHARK FAMILY TREE

Sharks have been hunting the oceans since before the time of the dinosaurs. Together with chimaeras and rays, they belong to a group of fish with a skeleton made from mineralized cartilage, rather than bone. About 500 shark species in nine main groups are around today, but many other sharklike fish that lived millions of years ago are now extinct.

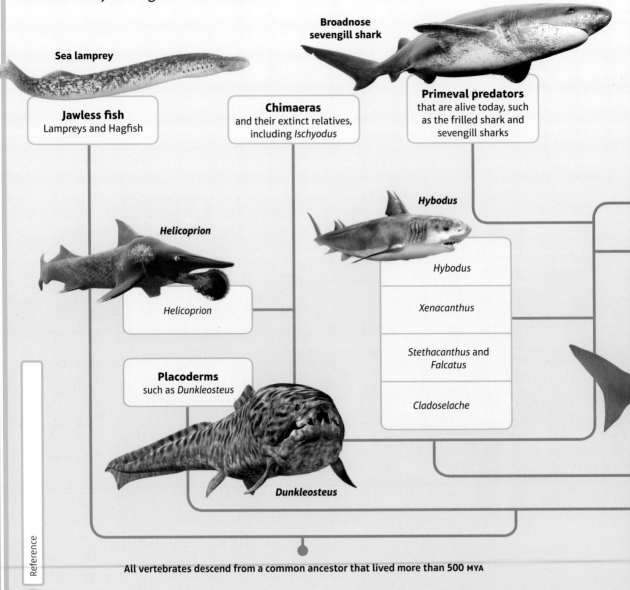

Sea lamprey

Broadnose sevengill shark

Jawless fish
Lampreys and Hagfish

Chimaeras
and their extinct relatives, including *Ischyodus*

Primeval predators
that are alive today, such as the frilled shark and sevengill sharks

Helicoprion

Hybodus

Helicoprion

| Hybodus |
| *Xenacanthus* |
| *Stethacanthus* and *Falcatus* |
| *Cladoselache* |

Placoderms
such as *Dunkleosteus*

Dunkleosteus

All vertebrates descend from a common ancestor that lived more than 500 MYA

Horn shark,
an example of a
bullhead shark

**Killers between
the tides** such as
wobbegongs and
bullhead sharks

**Open-ocean
cruisers and chasers**
such as the
great white shark

**Mud-rooting
monsters**
such as sawsharks and
angelsharks

**Muscle-mouthed
gulpers** such as the
whale shark and
the nurse shark

Devils of the dark
such as lantern sharks,
spiny dogfish, and
sleeper sharks

Inshore marauders
such as cat sharks
and reef sharks

THE EVIDENCE

Scientists use different methods to
work out how groups of animals
have evolved. They look for
similarities in living sharks and their
DNA, and study fossils of prehistoric
species. But cartilaginous skeletons
of sharks do not preserve well, and
fossilized teeth sometimes provide
the only evidence from the past.

7 in (18 cm)

Fossilized
Megalodon tooth

Rays

**Modern bony
fish and
other vertebrates**

Leedsichthys

Leedsichthys

***Acanthodes*, a
carboniferous
spiny "shark"**

Acanthodes

KEY

Living   Extinct

THE SHARK MACHINE

Most sharks are big, torpedo-shaped predators that swim through open water, but some have a flattened body for settling on the sea floor. A few others filter plankton from water instead of biting prey. Like most other fish, sharks have paired pectoral and pelvic fins for steering, and dorsal and anal fins for stabilizing the body's posture in the water. Power for movement comes from the shark's beating tail.

Skeleton
The spine and rest of the shark's skeleton is made from cartilage that is hardened by minerals. The skeleton of most other vertebrates is mainly made of bone, which is even harder.

Second dorsal fin is absent in some sharks

Tail
The spine runs upward into the top section (lobe) of the tail, which is usually bigger than the lower section.

Anal fin

Pelvic fin (one of a pair)

Skin
Shark skin feels rough like sandpaper, because it is covered with tiny, toothlike prickles called "dermal denticles."

Oily liver
Unlike most bony fishes, sharks do not have a gas-filled swim bladder to stay buoyant. Instead, buoyancy comes from an extra-oily liver.

Reference

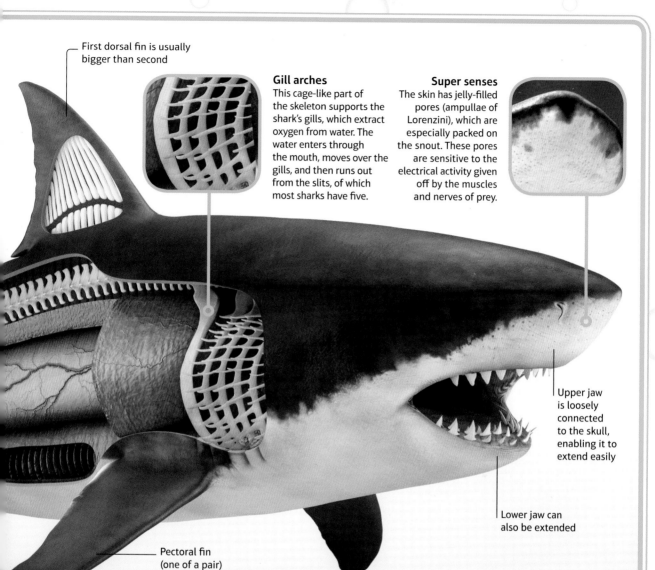

First dorsal fin is usually bigger than second

Gill arches
This cage-like part of the skeleton supports the shark's gills, which extract oxygen from water. The water enters through the mouth, moves over the gills, and then runs out from the slits, of which most sharks have five.

Super senses
The skin has jelly-filled pores (ampullae of Lorenzini), which are especially packed on the snout. These pores are sensitive to the electrical activity given off by the muscles and nerves of prey.

Upper jaw is loosely connected to the skull, enabling it to extend easily

Lower jaw can also be extended

Pectoral fin (one of a pair)

JAWS AND TEETH

Sharks are predators—some filter feed, while others use their jaws to bite into their prey. Some sharks can protrude their jaws further than others.

Cutting teeth of great white shark

Grinding teeth of bullhead shark

Projectile jaws of goblin shark

Gouging jaws of cookiecutter shark

SHARKS AS HUNTERS

All sharks get their food by eating other animals. A few, such as the whale shark, are filter-feeders, who strain tiny animals from the ocean's floating plankton. Other sharks scavenge on dead material and will even follow fishing boats to grab leftovers. However, most kinds of shark hunt, bite, and kill living prey. They have an impressive array of sense organs for hunting. The smallest sharks target fish and invertebrates, but some of the biggest hunters prey on animals up to the size of dolphins and seals.

MORE THAN ¹/₂ MILE (1 KM) AWAY

LESS THAN ¹/₂ MILE (1 KM) AWAY

Smelling the blood
Sharks can detect the presence of prey across miles of ocean water by using the super-sensitive smell and taste receptors in their nostrils and mouth. Some sharks are said to be able to sniff a drop of blood 3 miles (5 km) away.

Listening for movement
Sharks can hear the sound of an animal splashing about in the water, and some are good at homing in on the thrashing noises made by a so-called "feeding frenzy," in which lots of sharks gather to feast on meat.

Feeling the movement
A series of pores run in a so-called lateral line down the side of the shark's body. Seawater seeping into these pores goes through tiny tubes containing sensors that detect changing water currents, which are possible evidence of nearby prey.

DIFFERENT HUNTING TECHNIQUES

Many sharks are masters of the ambush and take their prey by surprise in dark or cloudy waters. Some hunters, such as angelsharks, rely on camouflage to stay hidden on the seabed. The so-called mackerel sharks, including the great white, are champion swimmers and chase down prey in open water. This great white has leapt out of water after prey.

50 FT (15 M) AWAY

3.3 FT (1 M) AWAY

Eyeing the victim
As the shark approaches its prey, its eyes form a clear image of the target. The eyes of some kinds of shark work well even at low light intensity, helping them hunt in dark or cloudy water.

Sensing the life
When a shark gets close, another kind of sensing system takes over—the ampullae of Lorenzini. The ampullae are jelly-filled pores concentrated on the snout that detect the faint electrical activity of the prey's muscles and nerves, even when it tries to hide.

Taking a bite
Unlike most other back-boned animals, the upper jaw of a shark is not rigidly attached to the skull, so the jaws can protrude outward. This helps the shark to take a more effective and bigger bite when it lunges forward to attack prey.

SHARK LIFE CYCLES

Most fish lay many eggs to improve the chances of survival of at least some of their tiny young. Sharks produce fewer offspring, and about 60 percent of species give birth to live pups, after a prolonged pregnancy. This means the pups are born at an advanced stage of development, giving them a good chance of looking after themselves. The remaining sharks produce eggs in protective, horny cases.

Some female sharks have given birth **without being fertilized**.

Gestation

Sharks that give birth to live young do so after a pregnancy that, depending upon species, may be up to two years long. In some kinds of shark, the unborn pups are even nourished by the mother in the womb.

Sharks that give birth to live young

Giving birth

Sharks often choose to give birth in sheltered nursery grounds, away from the danger of predators. This newborn lemon shark is still attached to its mother by its umbilical cord, the special thread that passed nutrients into the unborn pup when it was still in the womb.

Mating
All species of shark have internal fertilization so must mate. During mating, the male bites the female to hold on and then passes sperm into her body through special grooved structures on his pelvic fins.

Reference

GROWING UP

The habitat and even appearance of a shark can change as it grows up. Many newborn sharks spend their infancy in the shelter of shallow bays before venturing out into the deeper ocean. Young sharks of some species have striking patterns, possibly for camouflage. Zebra shark pups, for instance, lose their stripes and become spotted as they grow older. These stripes may help the pups look like sea snakes.

Zebra shark pup

Adult zebra shark

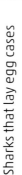

Sharks that lay egg cases

Egg cases

Some sharks produce leathery egg cases that harden soon after release. Some cases are ridged to help them get wedged between rocks, such as the spiral casing of this bullhead shark case. Others have tassels so they snag on weed and don't get washed away.

Growing in the egg case

Young get nourishment from their yolk sac and grow bigger inside their egg cases. The cases may take a year to hatch, but some kinds of shark retain them for longer in their body for protection, and only release them when their development is nearly complete.

SHARKS IN OCEAN HABITATS

With a few exceptions, all sharks live in the saltwater of the ocean. Some sharks, including the most primitive kinds, prefer to stick to deep, dark waters that make up the biggest proportion of the ocean habitat by volume. Others hunt near the surface, or stay in the shallower coastal waters of the ocean's continental shelves.

MIGRATION

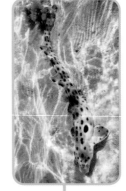

Some sharks are long-distance travelers, following migratory routes that may differ between age groups or sexes. Female blue sharks cross the Atlantic Ocean, between mating grounds in the west and sites for giving birth in the east.

Intertidal zone
0–66 ft (0–20 m)
Where the ocean meets the land, animals must cope with the movement of tides and the crashing of waves. A few sharks, such as the epaulette shark, can survive out of water while the tide is low.

Surface ocean waters
0–656 ft (0–200 m)
The clear, sunlit ocean surface supports billions of tiny animals and plants called plankton—food for filter-feeders such as whale sharks and forming the start of a food chain that ends with meat-eaters such as the great white.

Sunlight Zone
0–656 ft
(0–200 m)

Twilight Zone
656–3,280 ft
(200–1,000m)

Coastal ocean waters
0–656 ft (0–200 m)
Many sharks stick to the waters along the edges of continents and islands, where nutrient-rich waters can teem with prey. Females of some shark species, such as the lemon shark, give birth in shallow bays and lagoons.

Deep ocean waters
3,280–13,120 ft (1,000–4,000 m)
The deep ocean is home to bizarre animals, such as the frilled shark. Light dims into complete darkness at greater depths, through the gloom of the "twilight zone," the pitch blackness of the "midnight zone," to the "abyss" at the bottom.

Midnight Zone
3,280–13,120 ft
(1,000–4,000 m)

Abyss
13,120–19,680 ft
(4,000–6,000 m)

SHARK FACTS AND FIGURES

Sharks are dominant predators in the world's oceans—a place they share with a huge variety of animals. They have incredible, record-breaking lives. Impressive predators, the biggest meat-eating sharks are at the top of the ocean food chain.

SHARK HABITATS

- **Longest shark migration**: Great white shark (12,427 miles/20,000 km)
- **Longest vertical shark migration**: Pygmy shark (at least 4,920 ft/1,500 m)
- **Longest time survived out of water**: Blind shark (18 hours)
- **Deepest-living shark**: Portuguese dogfish (12,057 ft/3,675 m)
- **Shallowest-living shark**: Epaulette shark (sometimes barely submerged)
- **Smallest home range**: Blacktip reef shark (0.1 sq mile/0.3 sq km)

SHARK LIFE CYCLES

- **Longest-lived shark**: Spiny dogfish (maximum recorded age: 75 years)
- **Slowest growth rate**: Greenland shark (0.39 in/1 cm per year)
- **Fastest growth rate**: Whale shark (as a juvenile: 18 in/46 cm per year)

Biggest sharks shown to scale

Great white shark (16.4 ft/6 m)

Basking shark (33 ft/10 m)

0   16.4 ft (5 m)

THE SHARK MACHINE

- **Biggest shark to have ever lived**: *Megalodon* (66 ft/20 m long)
- **Biggest shark alive today**: Whale shark (66 ft/20 m long)
- **Second biggest shark alive today**: Basking shark (33 ft/10 m long)
- **Biggest meat-eating shark**: Great white shark (19.6 ft/6 m long)
- **Smallest shark**: Dwarf lantern shark (8.2 in/21 cm long)
- **Longest tail relative to size**: Thresher shark (half of total length)
- **Thickest skin of any animal**: Whale shark (6 in/15 cm)

SHARKS AS HUNTERS

- **Strongest bite of any animal**: Great white shark (18,000 Newtons; a Newton is a measurement of force—the force of a bite in this case)
- **Strongest shark bite for its size**: Horn shark (338 Newtons)
- **Fastest bite**: Wobbegong ($\frac{1}{50}$ second)
- **Biggest shark teeth ever**: *Megalodon* (7 in/18 cm long)
- **Biggest shark teeth of any shark alive today**: Great white shark (2.7 in/7 cm)
- **Biggest teeth relative to size**: Large-toothed cookiecutter shark
- **Fastest swimming shark**: Short-finned mako shark (62 mph/100 kph)
- **Slowest swimming shark**: Greenland shark (0.7 mph/1.25 kph)

Megalodon
(66 ft/20 m)

Whale shark
(66 ft/20 m)

49.2 ft (15 m)

66 ft (20 m)

GLOSSARY

Anal fin
An unpaired fin on the underside of a fish, behind the pelvic fins and in front of the tail.

Antenna
A feeler-like sense organ on the head of certain kinds of invertebrate (animals without a backbone).

Barbel
A whisker-like, sensory organ near the mouth of certain kinds of fish, such as the sawshark.

Bioluminescence
The production of light by living things, caused by chemical reactions in the body. Many deep-sea animals are luminous (produce light), which helps them attract prey, distract predators, or communicate.

Bivalve
A shelled mollusk with a shell made up of two connected parts. Clams and mussels are bivalves.

Buoyancy
The ability of an aquatic (water-living) living thing to float in water.

Camouflage
The way the appearance of an animal, such as its color or shape, helps it blend in with its surroundings.

Cartilage
A tough, rubbery material that makes up the skeleton of sharks and related fish. Most other vertebrates (back-boned animals) have a skeleton made mainly of bone with a little cartilage in places.

Cold-blooded
An animal whose body temperature varies with that of the surroundings. Reptiles, amphibians, fish, and invertebrates are cold-blooded.

Continental shelf
A region of shallow ocean water that surrounds a continent. On its outer edge, it plunges down into the deep sea.

Crustacean
An invertebrate with jointed legs and, usually, a hard, outer shell. Shrimp, crabs, lobsters, and krill are crustaceans.

Denticle
A tiny, hard, toothlike scale on the skin of sharks and rays.

Dorsal fin
An unpaired upright fin on the back of a fish, whale, or dolphin.

Echinoderm
An invertebrate with a starlike body, hard chalky plates in its skin, and tube feet. Starfish and sea urchins are echinoderms.

Egg case
A tough, protective, horny casing that encloses the fertilized eggs of some sharks and rays.

Feeding frenzy
When a group of predators, such as sharks, gathers together to herd and attack prey.

Filter-feeder
An animal that feeds by straining out plankton or other small particles of food suspended in water.

Flatfish
A type of bony fish in which both eyes have moved to the same side of the head by the time it has become an adult. It then lives with its "blind side" facing downward close to the seabed. Plaice and flounders are flatfish.

Food chain
A sequence in which energy in food passes from one living thing to another, such as when plants are eaten by herbivores, and herbivores are eaten by carnivores.

Fossil
The remains or traces of long-extinct animals or plants left in rocks.

Gill
A part of the body used by an animal to breathe in water.

DK Delhi
Senior Editor Sreshtha Bhattacharya
Editor Agnibesh Das
Design Team Kshitiz Dobhal, Ranjita Bhattacharji
Senior DTP Designer Harish Aggarwal
DTP Designers Jaypal Singh, Syed Md Farhan
Picture Researcher Nishwan Rasool
Jacket Designer Dhirendra Singh
Managing Jackets Editor Saloni Singh
Pre-production Manager Balwant Singh
Production Manager Pankaj Sharma
Picture Research Manager Taiyaba Khatoon
Managing Editor Kingshuk Ghoshal
Managing Art Editor Govind Mittal

DK London
Senior Editor Chris Hawkes
Senior Art Editor Spencer Holbrook
US Editor Rebecca Warren
Jacket Editor Claire Gell
Jacket Designer Natalie Godwin
Jacket Design Development Manager Sophia MTT
Producer, Pre-production Robert Dunn
Producer Vivienne Yong
Managing Art Editor Philip Letsu
Publisher Andrew Macintyre
Associate Publishing Director Liz Wheeler
Art Director Karen Self
Publishing Director Jonathan Metcalf

Written by Derek Harvey
Consultant: Dr. Kim Bryan

First American Edition, 2016
Published in the United States by DK Publishing
1745 Broadway, 20th Floor, New York NY 10019

Copyright © 2016 Dorling Kindersley Limited
DK, a Division of Penguin Random House LLC
23 15 14 13
019–291131–Jun/2016

A catalog record for this book is available from
the Library of Congress.
ISBN: 978-1-4654-5084-5

DK books are available at special discounts when
purchased in bulk for sales promotions, premiums,
fund-raising, or educational use. For details,
contact: DK Publishing Special Markets,
1745 Broadway, 20th Floor, New York NY 10019
SpecialSales@dk.com

Printed and bound in China

For the curious
www.dk.com

This book was made with Forest Stewardship
Council™ certified paper – one small step
in DK's commitment to a sustainable future.
For more information go to
www.dk.com/our-green-pledge

SHARKS
AND OTHER DEADLY
OCEAN CREATURES

VISUAL ENCYCLOPEDIA

Oxygen in the water moves into the blood in the gills.

Intertidal zone
The region of ocean shoreline that is regularly uncovered and then covered by water during the ebb and flow of the tide.

Invertebrate
An animal without a backbone.

Keel
A ridge running down each side of the body near the tail, in some kinds of fish. Keels help stabilize the fish in the water and are prominent in fast swimmers.

Larva
The young stage of certain kinds of animal. Usually a larva looks different from the adult form.

Mammal
A back-boned, warm-blooded animal, such as a human or whale. Mothers of all mammals feed their young with milk.

Migration
A periodic animal journey, usually to reach feeding or breeding grounds. Many ocean animals migrate across stretches of ocean, but others do vertical migration from the depths of the ocean to its surface.

Mollusk
An invertebrate with a soft, muscular body. Some mollusks, such as snails and clams, have a hard shell. Others, such as squid and octopuses, do not.

Operculum
A flap that covers the gill openings in most kinds of fish. It is not found in sharks and rays, which is why their gill slits are visible.

Parasite
A living thing that gets food or shelter from another, called the host, causing the other harm.

Pectoral fin
A pair of fins connected to the "chest" region of a fish, usually just behind the head.

Pelvic fin
A pair of fins connected to the underside of a fish, behind the pectoral fins and usually in the region of the belly.

Photosynthesis
A chemical process in plants, algae, and seaweed in which sunlight is used to make food from carbon dioxide and water.

Plankton
Tiny animals and plants that swim or float in water.

Polyp
A tiny, anemone-like, moving part of a coral. Each polyp has stinging tentacles for grabbing prey.

Predator
An animal that kills another animal for food.

Prey
An animal that is killed by a predator for food.

Spiracle
A small breathing hole behind the eyes of most sharks and rays. Some of the water taken into the mouth for breathing emerges through the spiracles; the rest moves out over the gills.

Reef
A large, rocky structure, usually found around tropical coastlines, which is formed by the growth of coral.

Reptile
A back-boned, cold-blooded animal with dry, scaly skin. Turtles, lizards, snakes, and crocodiles are reptiles.

Scavenger
An animal that gets its food by eating the leftovers of other animals.

Tentacle
Long, soft, moving "arms" in some kinds of animal, including octopuses and squid. They use the tentacles to catch prey.

Venom
A poisonous substance that harms the body when it enters through a bite or a sting.

Vertebrate
An animal with a backbone. Examples include fish, amphibians, reptiles, birds, and mammals.

Warm-blooded
An animal whose body temperature stays warm, even when the surroundings are cold. Mammals and birds are warm-blooded. A few fish, such as the great white and sailfish, are partly warm-blooded too.

INDEX